HC

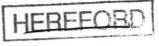

A Flight
of Arrows

A Flight of Arrows

Opinions, people, places

Alan Sillitoe

ROBSON BOOKS

First published in Great Britain in 2003 by Robson Books,
The Chrysalis Building, Bramley Road, London W10 6SP

An imprint of Chrysalis Books Group plc

Typeset by FiSH Books, London WC1
Printed in Great Britain by Creative Print & Design (Wales), Ebbw Vale

Contents

Acknowledgements

'Joseph Conrad' was published in French, in *europe* (*revue littéraire mensuelle*) in 1980. British Council: New Writing (2001).

'On the Picaresque Novel and the Picaresque Hero' was published first as 'L'Esprit du Herós Picaresque' in 1981, in *hi/cran* no. 17, Amiens. In 1983 it was published in English by Bernard Stone's *Turret Papers*, no. 2.

'Great Expectations' was an introduction to the novel in Oxford World's Classics, 1999.

'D H Lawrence and District' was first published in *D. H. Lawrence,* edited by Stephen Spender and published by Weidenfeld and Nicolson, 1973.

'Robert Tressell' was written as an introduction to the Panther paperback of 1965.

'Arnold Bennett: The Man from the North' was written as an introduction to *The Old Wives' Tale* (Pan Books, 1964).

'Robert Graves' Centenary', 1995, was given as a talk on the BBC *Today Programme*, 1998.

'Ted Hughes' was published in the *Guardian* at the time of his death, and then included in a Faber anthology devoted to the poet.

'Maps and the Great War' was written as an introduction to *The Topography of Armageddon* by Peter Chasseud, 1991.

'Government Forms' appeared in *The Times*, 1971.

'Politics' was printed in the *New Statesman*, 1992.

'Coalminers: Everything to Lose', was first published in German, in *Der Magazin* in Zurich. The first publication in English was in the *Evansville Review*, Vol. X, 2999, in the United States.

'The Confessions of a Smoking Monster' appeared in *The Times*, 1977.

'Sport and Nationalism' is taken from my first selection of essays *Mountains and Caverns* (1975) but rewritten.

'St Pagoire and the Anniversary of the Revolution' was published in the *Guardian*, 1989.

'The Retreat from Mons' was published in the *Guardian*, 1990.

'Robbed!' Also published in the *Guardian*, 1990.

Guardian Diary Piece – the *Guardian*, 1990.

'Up the Rigi' – printed in German, in *Der Magazin*, Zurich, 2000.

'Incomparable Derbyshire', *New York Herald Tribune* travel section, 1984.

'To St Catherine's Monastery' was published in the *Geographical Magazine* in 1980.

'Colonel Patterson the Zionist' was published in the *Jewish Quarterly*, 1978.

Preface

Whenever I am faced with a preface (or foreword or introduction) I ignore it and go straight to the text. If and when the book is finished I might return to those few pages at the beginning in the hope (in some cases) of enlightenment as to what it was all about. The reader here may feel free to do the same, though this preface will be kept as short as possible.

My autobiography *Life Without Armour* (1995) closed in the year 1962. This book makes a kind of reconnoitering continuation, and gives some idea as to what happened since. Most pieces have already been published in magazines and newspapers, but even so have needed such intensive rewriting that I wonder at editors having printed them. They are therefore quite new and, I hope, hardly recognisable from what they were before. Non-fiction (like fiction, only more so) should run effortlessly, the wheels not heard to creak and squeak as the vehicle goes along.

Selection has been difficult from scores of pieces written and published over the years, and there is no knowing if those left out aren't more interesting than the ones put in. Decision-making is the writer's bane, since he must decide in everything (often after much anguish and uncertainty) whether or not the word is suitable in the phonetic scheme of the sentence.

I call this book *Flight of Arrows*, and though Nimrod – the mighty hunter before the Lord – shot an arrow into the sky to find out if God really did exist, and saw blood on the arrow when it came down as living proof that He did, yet was not killed for the impertinence, I don't expect any of these writings to have such a dramatic effect. Yet it is a flight of arrows, all the same.

Alan Sillitoe, 2003

A Flight of Arrows

A noise from the past, which cannot be ignored, comes as if out of a waking dream as I lean my bicycle against a fence, and look into a meadow that was once a battlefield. A simple explanation of the echo is elusive, but I eventually recall how, at the age of seventeen, one evening after work in the factory, I went into a cinema to see Laurence Olivier in *Henry V*.

The film was dedicated to the men of the British Airborne Division, which had been almost annihilated at Arnhem in the autumn of 1944. This gesture, well understood at the time, may not have been much recompense for the defeat, because one had since learned that the fiasco was due to bad weather, faulty intelligence (of all sorts) and inferior radio sets, which weren't able to make urgent messages readable.

The sacrifice of the Polish Parachute Brigade, and the capture of the bridge at Nijmegen by the US Army, redeemed the situation only insofar as it saved some of the British soldiers cut off north of the Rhine. The strategical concept was sound enough on paper, but the defeat was due, above all, to the Dutch Resistance leader Lindemans, who was working for the Germans, and betrayed to them the area of the landings some days beforehand. Had it not been for this treachery the war might have ended six months earlier.

It is not surprising that the film following this dedication was more successful than that battle, since the scale was smaller and the danger minimal. Laurence Olivier acted the king, and William Shakespeare had written the first draft screenplay over three hundred years before.

Armies were smaller in 1415, and such contact as existed between the commander and his warriors could hardly have been arranged by Montgomery for 'Operation Market Garden', though he was said to have done his best in this respect. In the Middle Ages the relationship between king and common soldier was more immediate and often brutal, while a modern general needs to be bureaucratic, distant and correct. One could say that the Battle of Agincourt succeeded for the British partly because of the rapport between King Harry and his army.

I didn't go to the sort of school where time was spent deciphering the writ of Shakespeare. A tale or two read aloud from Charles and Mary Lamb's stories of the plays was the most we were privileged to hear, though the teachers who intoned them deserved all credit for trying such works on us. Failure was fairly certain, because all we gathered was that Shakespeare, as one of my friends said at the time (in language recalled as positively Shakespearean) 'was all about the antics of sissy courtiers running around palaces sticking swords in each other'. Language that only sounded English from a distance was not something even the brightest could take in. The plain prose of Robert Louis Stevenson, Rider Haggard and Arthur Conan Doyle was all that our attention would accept.

With films, an advance into the world of Shakespeare became possible, at least for those who had the curiosity to find out more. The magnificently staged conflict of Agincourt showed a way in, with an awakening of intelligence by emotion or, at worst, the accumulation of understanding through atavistic delight.

If the visual effects of the battle were amazing, then the noise – and Walton's music – and the music itself of that massive flight of arrows against the advancing French cavalry was even more so. Whether dozing after a day's work, or deliciously involved with your girlfriend on the back row, there was no missing the sound, which reverberated against all four flock-papered walls of the musty cinema. Carried up to the ceiling of ornate mouldings as well and, you might have thought, spilling out onto the street, it went on and on, and ended all too soon because, like an orgasm, you wanted it to go on forever.

The importance of that moment was only half comprehended, but the effect had made a beginning, for some at least – a very few, perhaps, but for me a gradual understanding of the language was helped by seeing the film more than once, until the words began to make sense, and Shakespeare did not sound so unintelligible after all. The book of the film was cheap, because for ten shillings one could buy not only the script of *Henry V* but 36 others that Shakespeare had written, and go on to read those as well.

Perhaps I exaggerate, but the jump from bafflement to clarity can be compared to that of a foreigner acquiring enough of the language to take in a play he had loved at first hearing. The difference between my spoken English and Shakespeare's language of so long ago was wide enough, but love leaps all obstacles and distances, while infatuation – that needle-pointed arrowhead of the subconscious – is even speedier, and turns into undying love.

Mulling on that decisive flight of arrows brings to mind another autumn battle, in 1914, when the British Army was deployed on the high ground east of Ypres (or Wipers, as that ill-fated place came to be known to soldiers who suffered there, or to their relatives who received telegrams of their demise). The survivors of the battle, which went on for weeks, came to be called 'The Old Contemptibles', because the German Kaiser had referred to the British divisions as 'a contemptible little army'. They fought to stop several German army corps reaching the French coast and dividing one ally from another, and success for the Germans could have been so complete that from then on we might have had to believe that our very own and precious Shakespeare was of German birth!

Shakespeare was none other than one of us, so it is easy not to care who or what he was. Generally accepted assumptions must be accorded their validity, while realising all too well that 'patriotism is the last refuge of the scoundrel'. If my language

3

were to be threatened I would fight to the death to preserve it, on the other hand not forgetting that humour is always the last defence before taking to arms.

The German Army attributed its failure to break through at Ypres to the fact that each British battalion possessed dozens of machine guns, whereas there were but two to a battalion. The British infantry had been trained to fire their .303 Short Lee Enfield rifles, with an effective range of a thousand yards, at fifteen aimed shots a minute, so a full battalion could let go fifteen thousand rounds in that time, the equivalent of thirty machine guns at the rate of those days. The German mistake is therefore understandable.

Several of those German divisions that failed to break through consisted mainly of high school volunteers led by their officer-teachers, intelligent youngsters who wanted their chance of glory but were killed or wounded in their thousands, a massacre of the innocents.

In 1914 the British were helping to save France instead of subdue it, unlike five hundred years before at Agincourt, when it was the English who were trying to get to the Channel coast, and those flights of arrows were let loose with the same speed and dexterity of their descendants with rifles around Ypres.

That blanketing cloud of arrows, created by the lowliest of men using the cheapest of weapons since David the shepherd wielded his sling against Goliath, put paid to the nobleman on horseback, defeated this version of the medieval tank, and destroyed the 'flower of French chivalry'. The contest made sense to an entranced juvenile in the cinema, as did King Henry's rousing speech to his men before the battle. The 'antics of sissy courtiers running around palaces sticking swords in each other' were redeemed by his exhortations to fight and, if necessary, die – especially when, in the event, so few of them did. It was the kind of war, and he was the sort of king, that one could appreciate at seventeen.

One sat through the last scene of the king's courtship of Katharine because the touching speech on the devastation of France was a topical issue, since we all knew who had ruined that country (not to say almost the whole of Europe) in the previous five years.

It was no accident, then, that the first Shakespeare plays I read were *Henry V* and *Hamlet*, just as I tackled my first novels much earlier on hearing them dramatised on the BBC, which says a lot for the educational influence of the media.

Shakespeare had an effect on others, apart from the young and semi-literate. Artists, like fishes, feed off each other, and some wax wonderfully on the diet. Composers assiduously used his plays as inspiration for their music. Hector Berlioz, at 26, wrote a dramatic fantasy with chorus on *The Tempest*, but a violent cloudburst over Paris on the day of its first performance prevented people getting to the concert hall, which stayed almost empty. Stoical Berlioz could only comment, though with some chagrin, that the piece was 'washed down the drain'.

On another occasion, recovering in Nice from the devastating effects of a broken engagement, Berlioz was arrested by the King of Sardinia's police on a charge of spying, but got out of it by insisting, truthfully enough, that he was writing an overture for *King Lear*. He was 'ravaged day and night by a Shakespearean love', and in 1824 saw *Hamlet* at the age of 21. He was 'struck like a thunderbolt'. Five years later he married Harriet Smithson, who had played Ophelia.

Voltaire expressed a different view, though why should one expect the great to be less cantankerous than anybody else?

> 'That ape of genius sent
> By Satan among men to do his work.'

On a cycling tour of northern France, by the battlefield of Agincourt itself, scenes from the film came back vividly: the long wait of the soldiers through the rainy night, and the speech before the battle, then a look into the clouded sky clearing slowly after rain. The *katyusha* launch of arrows was not mentioned in the text, but Shakespeare excites even more intensely when something beyond what he created comes into the imagination. If the quality of his genius is ragged at the edges, those edges are golden. Like all great writers he can be read and enjoyed by everyone, whatever their race, sex, education, religion or even age. He is also an eternal inspiration to poets and composers, and to those lesser writers all of us must be. So much for that magic flight of arrows.

The Book

One of my earliest memories is of going to school at the age of five, of my sister leading me by the hand into a red-bricked three-storeyed structure on the edge of an area of slums in which we lived. The building is still there, over sixty years later, and used now as an electrical goods storehouse. The classroom backed onto a canal, and through the window we sometimes saw a horse pulling a laden barge. A main road ran along the front.

Every morning – maybe to keep the gang of little scruffs quiet, but, I like to think, from a policy of treating even such children with a sort of hopeful respect – the teacher read from the Bible. One did not question being pitched into a totally different world. It simply was. Those sonorous and rhythmical phrases called up landscapes of mountains and rivers, palm trees and bulrushes, of a sea that withdrew to enable the People chosen by God to write the Bible to walk over on dry land. Our teacher's commentaries were plain, but interesting.

Such images of places we had never seen, and had no hope of seeing, could not have been more different to the dilapidated townscape round about, many of whose houses were shortly to be bulldozed away. The young woman teacher read to us about God creating the heavens and the earth when up to that moment we hadn't thought to wonder where the world came from or how it was made, and certainly not the reason for our being on its surface.

She narrated the story of Abraham and Isaac, of the travels of Noah's family and all the animals in the ark, of how the Israelites had to work under the wicked taskmasters in Egypt, and then of Moses leading his people on forty years of hard wandering across the wilderness, to a sight of the Promised Land before he died. She would occasionally tell the stories in her own words, and read the text later. We learned that Saul and Jonathan in their deaths were not divided, and that even the mighty must fall.

Whether or not all of what she read from her own black leather-bound copy of the King James translation was immediately understood, I enjoyed the sombre diction in which the stories unrolled. She intoned the Commandments from Exodus and Deuteronomy over and over, so that if we couldn't easily recite them back at least we would always have some notion as to what was right and what was wrong – whatever rights and wrongs we were going on to commit.

It would be an exaggeration to say I was an avid reader of the Bible throughout childhood, but much was read at school in the time allotted. Another advantage of the Bible was that none of it was abridged or bowdlerised in any way. Spanning the generations, no discrimination was made as to the age of the reader.

Another early influence came from the cinema. I remember a Hollywood 'B' picture based on the life of the Victorian prime minister Benjamin Disraeli. During a debate in the House of Commons, Disraeli appeared to be asleep, while the Leader of the Opposition – probably Mr Gladstone – went through his oration. I supposed he didn't care to be influenced by whatever his adversary had to say. Such a mark of self-assurance (which may have been a mannerism to confound his enemies, and in any case could have been put in by the scriptwriters) made an impression; my temperament found such a tactic congenial.

Not to be particularly interested in what his opponent had to say showed the action of an individual who had faith in himself and his ideas. This, I thought, is the way to deal with anyone who might try to tell me what I do not think it is worthwhile to believe. The words of the great poet King David may already have been

8

noted in glancing through the Bible: 'Let them be ashamed and confounded that seek after my soul: let them be turned backwards and put to confusion that desire my hurt.'

As a teenager during the Second World War I became interested in everything to do with Russia, taking out any book from the local branch library with the name of that country in its title. Even a collection of folk tales did not escape my searching fingers, in which was a story of how the Devil comes to a village and addresses the peasants, promising that any man will be entitled to keep whatever land he can walk around in a single day.

The greedy and optimistic set out to walk, in the burning month of August, a greater distance than ever before in their lives, and all fell dead or exhausted before completing any kind of circuit. The only person to end with a reasonable area of land was a Jew, who finished his perambulation before the sun reached its zenith.

If the story was meant to be anti-Semitic – and I suppose that in part it was – the intention was lost on me. I could only ruminate on how intelligent and worthy of emulation the wise man was, while hoping I would have acted in the same way.

Before going out to work at fourteen I was called onto the stage in the assembly hall by the headmaster. I wondered what I could have done wrong, but I need not have worried. The benign man shook my hand, and gave me a copy of the same sort of Bible read to me on my first day at school. Perhaps it was a reward for my better-than-average essays, but an inscription inside said that it was: 'Awarded for Proficiency in Biblical Knowledge'.

It proved a good book to take into the world, and I still have it on my shelf although all others of the period are lost. I've since read it more than once, from Genesis to Malachi, or from Genesis to Second Chronicles in the Masoretic layout. Always within hands' reach, the book even travelled on active service with me to Malaya. Something of a talisman, it grew into a place of refuge, became a book of memory for being with me over half a century, and it is valued as much for the system of ethics it extols as for the stories and the style in which they are told.

Why the mysterious and separate world became so much part of me I'll never know, except that it could not have been otherwise. Most evenings these days, after finishing my writing, I read a chapter or two (on my way through yet again) so as to settle my spirit for sleep. A person once looked surprised on my saying I had been reading the Bible in this way while writing *Saturday Night and Sunday Morning.*

The school prize was rarely consulted during my years in the factory, because the war was on, all interest taken up by what was happening on the battlefronts. A man stood at the factory gates preaching Communism, and his pamphlets told of German atrocities in Russia.

I was off work only once during that time. Almost too weak to get out of bed because of the 'flu, my mother told me to see Dr Lowenthal who was, she said, a refugee from Germany. He had a good reputation in the district.

On a freezing morning I walked through the streets to his house, and in the surgery, with me still wearing overalls in case he said I was fit enough to go straight back to work, he asked what was wrong. I announced that I didn't feel too good, to which he responded, with a smile and in his strong accent: 'No, you don't look very good, either.'

I suddenly felt much better at the state of my health being taken seriously yet in a semi-jocular fashion. From that moment I became less a sick animal and more of a human being, pleased to have confirmation that I was not malingering – such was the sense of failure at being off work.

I wanted to get into the war as soon as possible, apart from helping to make munitions. A newspaper article said that recruits were needed for the Air Training Corps. When I applied to join, the adjutant of the squadron, Flying Officer Pink, lined up a group of us, and commanded those who did not brush their teeth every morning to raise a hand. Mine was one of them, and I don't imagine anyone other than Jack Pink, with his hortatory requests, could have made me use a toothbrush from so early on. It was his vocation to get the best from us in the next four years, and he certainly did. The realisation that he was Jewish came because he was the one officer who didn't accompany us on the infrequent church parades.

Reading matter came out of technical manuals on navigation, meteorology and mathematics. My English improved, much spare time being devoted to acquiring a kind of secondary education. I wanted – and the sooner the better – to become a competent navigator in one of those hundreds of aircraft going night after night to unload the wrath of God onto Nazi Germany, a country which – having sown the wind – was having to reap the whirlwind. At such a time it was them or us, and the confidence of being on the right side was an inalienable part of me.

As a reader I became attracted to travel guidebooks, fascinated by their coloured maps of foreign countries. During my dinner hour, after a shilling meal at a British Restaurant, I would bike into town for a quick look along the shelves of a secondhand bookshop. For sixpence I bought a first edition (1876) of Baedeker's *Palestine and Syria*. The year must have been 1944, and I took it on my first trip to Israel thirty years later, together with Zev Vilnay's up-to-date guidebook.

When I came home from work one evening near the end of the war, my mother opened the newspaper before putting my food on the table, to show me a double-page spread of pictures from Belsen. No one had known the real extent of what had happened in Europe – at least, we didn't. Even if we had read *The Times* instead of the *Daily Mirror* we might not have been more accurately informed. She leaned over my shoulder: 'Just you look at what the Germans have done to people.'

Few could imagine that the enemy and their willing helpers had murdered millions of men, women and children because they were Jewish. I did not take in that the heaps of bodies were those of Jews, perhaps because the newspaper text wasn't there, though I soon learned from other sources.

One felt pity for the victims, and rage at a phenomenon beyond all understanding. Books and documents, films and memoirs eventually came my way, as well as meetings with some who had survived the experience. I become, if possible, more affected by such revelations the older I get, and sometimes wonder at what point the clock of history could be turned back and set onto another course so that the Holocaust would not have happened.

In his book *God's First Love*, the Austrian Catholic theologian Friedrich Heer analysed the relationship of Jews and Christians over two thousand years, and examined the attitude of the church to the mass murder of Jews during that time, discussing its responsibility for what happened in the twentieth century. Even the most unknowing should realise that if the Jews are persecuted one day it will be the turn of others – and maybe yourself – the next. Toleration of one's neighbour may be the lowest common denominator of self-preservation but, as the Bible emphasises, it is the only one to live by.

Such reflections may seem far from the influence on me of the Bible, yet are relevant to it. During the process of becoming a writer I read something that applied to the vocation. In the fourth chapter of Exodus, Moses said to God that he was not eloquent enough to talk to the people, that he was slow of speech and of a slow tongue. The Lord said to him: 'Who hath made man's mouth? Or who maketh the dumb or deaf, or the seeing, or the blind? Is not Aaron the Levite thy brother? I know that he can speak well. And thou shalt speak unto him, and put words in his mouth; and I will be with thy mouth, and with his mouth . . . And he shall be thy spokesman unto the people: and he shall be, even he shall be to thee, instead of a mouth.'

At the risk of being sacrilegious, such a mechanism can be likened to inspiration. A writer needs words to be put into his mouth or onto the tip of his pen from a source unknown. He imagines them as part of his own voice, words he will use to make sure that what he writes is as close as possible to the human condition.

One learns from the Bible that if you believe in God at all, He is the one who is concerned for the people He creates and continually creates. Those characters that you delineate as a writer must be regarded with compassion, the villains as well as the

12

heroes. However tragic the theme of a novel, you should never leave the reader at the end thinking that life is not worth living.

In this respect at least, the Bible played a large part in civilising me.

10 January 1999

On the Picaresque Novel and the Picaresque Hero

'The Mentality of the Picaresque Hero' was written as a kind of tuning fork for two novels – *A Start in Life* (1970) and its sequel *Life Goes On* (1985). Such reflections propelled the plot forward, and kept the tone, much of which was culled from those earlier works of the picaresque by Mateo Aleman and Alain LeSage. I wanted to write a modern picaresque novel (I ended up doing two, and maybe a third) shadowed by the works of those great masters.

Life is brief, and the picaresque hero knows it more than most. The true hero, statuesque rather than picaresque, knows it least. The picaro acts as if he is going to die tomorrow, while the true hero lords it as if he will live forever. The picaro, in other words, wants everything today. He craves to escape into the world of reality from youthful fantasy, but never quite gets there. The picaro is both the dreamer and the man of action, but his dreams are not so intense that they keep him from action, nor his actions so deeply considered that they destroy his dreams.

The picaro's character can vary, because though his clear goals occasionally seem like ambition, he is often consumed by false ambitions that are no more than goals. Such impulses eventually lead to a feeling for ambition but, more often than not, they lead to disaster. Though he may have no clear notion as to what his ambition might be, he feels that only quick advantage can take him closer to obtaining it.

There are no disasters to a picaro, only setbacks, and he will do anything to further his schemes. He has a will to succeed rather than any well-defined path in life, and he will pursue his way by all the charm and guile of his nature. He will not do so by work. Sufficient people already labour to maintain an opulent world for him to enjoy, and there is no place for our hero in an occupation that from the outset would seem both disagreeable and tedious. In any case, not altogether uncharitably, our hero knows that for him to work would mean taking bread out of the mouths of others. Modesty would, in this instance and no other, lead him to protest that bread of so little value can only be scorned.

Adaptable and intelligent, the picaro looks upon work as something which would not allow him to display and exploit the full range of his peculiar genius. From the point of view of the picaresque hero no values in the world appear to be stable. If he is a born thief it is merely to acquire money quickly, which after all is only earning it but as in a film speeded up.

He is also a born thief of ideas, when he needs them, because to devise any philosophy or justification for his actions would only lead to the discovery, when they were put to the test, that someone had propagated them before him.

Therefore he is a conservative, believing in the basic order of society, so that he can learn all the rules and know better how to exist, otherwise he would vanish forever.

Within the limits, rough as they may be, the world is a merry-go-roundabout, and he is at that calm place in the middle from which he jumps onto the spinning part, with all its prize-like glitter and colour, or opportune moments to brag, cheat or seduce. He leaps off the roundabout when it becomes too fast and threatening for comfort, back to his centre island of safety, on realising that outside it are no secure places for him.

He must have a refuge from the perils of the world, and sometimes it exists only within himself. That is the frailest refuge of all, which he can hardly bear to be in, since it contains so little to support him. Better to be outside, rather than rely on interior resources. The kind of life he is temperamentally fitted to pursue is often harsh, but as long as the danger does not come too often, it is tolerable because, as a picaro, he can usually change things at least temporarily for the better.

If we were to define the picaresque tale, one chapter would describe how a temporarily destitute young itinerant came to an evening campfire over which a pot of succulent stew was cooking. He would tell a story, which could only be what is known as picaresque. In the tale he would have no time to develop character, or style, or indulge in prolonged research. The hero of his tale – like himself – has to be young, good looking, witty, brave (to a degree) and daring, as well as sexually potent and promiscuous. In short, he must have many of the qualities that the people around the campfire, in charge of the provisions, cannot possibly possess.

The hero has certain disadvantages in that he does not know his parents (or one of them) and so believes himself to be a bastard. He has been cast off without resources because his petty crimes can no longer be tolerated, an event which he, however, puts down to a malign fate.

He has little education, though much aptitude for acquiring a gold-leaf veneer of sophistication – like the kind which, when painted on someone at a sumptuous Renaissance feast, kills them because the skin is eventually unable to breathe. Lack of diligence has sharpened his wits. Having no set aim in life gives him freedom of manoeuvre. Such advantages engender optimism. He never lacks energy. He develops diplomacy and cunning.

When he tells his story by the campfire, after an adventure in which the above qualities availed him nothing, he relates his life-story to the rich travellers but stops at the point where it will be necessary to explain why the last adventure failed, and lets it be known that he cannot go on until he is given the best of meat and drink.

They fall under his spell, and while imbibing, our hero eyes the glitter and panoply of the parked caravan, or the lures of the fixed settlement around him. But the appurtenances of civilisation are not for him, not even to stay with for a while, or accompany a few miles down the road. He is a rover, an observer, a tale-teller and confidence man – the artist without an art except for the expertise of occasionally getting what he wants.

Being born without that adult ability of buckling down to the dull plod of making a living in some established trade or profession, he is of no fixed value to society. He cannot then be a rival to the people he is both entertaining and sponging off. He is affected by a subtle and incurable illness that will never let him know peace. Even when the well of fortune stops in his favour he cannot keep still and enjoy what he has got, either because the danger has thereby increased and he must escape, or because, by feeling that he can acquire still more riches, he overreaches himself in his greed and loses all. A gambler who is not content till he has gained heaven often ends up by losing the warmth of hell as well.

Every established trader in the caravan, every settled professor or solid bureaucrat, or prosperous self-satisfied preacher, each of whom is slowly accumulating fame or wealth (or both) has a side to him that warms to the picaro's tale.

The yarn is spun out of his own backbone. A wandering no-good thief has many tales to tell. When not narrating he is acting out his falsehoods and exaggerations. Nothing daunts him.

He may be in tatters, wounded, starving after a series of misadventures that he brought on himself by unwise and precipitate behaviour, but his face is bright, his gestures cool, his words seducing. He can go from rags to opulence in a night by a chance meeting with a gullible priest, generous nobleman or warm-hearted widow – or the other way with more alarming rapidity. He is the epitome of life with the lid off where, but for the grace of God, go all. Despair is not for him, since it would rob him of the energy to pursue the kind of life that has chosen him for its victim.

He finds his way out of any labyrinth because he is God's plaything, but he never knows the grace of God. God is for those who believe in the superiority of the spirit, the necessity of ethics, the comfort of morals. While they pray, he preys on them, without whom he would have no existence. He is the devil on two sticks, the spirit of anarchy, which resides in everyone. Neither would they exist without him. He is the open prison-window of themselves, and acts as if there is no tomorrow in a world that lives as if the day after tomorrow was worth waiting for. That is his strength, because he will live for as long as the world goes on.

By middle age the picaro must have established his identity, made or married into a fortune, and reconciled himself to the life of a gentleman. He is no longer a picaro. If atrophy or boredom get the upper hand he loses all, descending into oblivion and beggary. Age kills off our picaresque hero, but there is always another to take his place.

The picaro has existed in all ages, and it is the novelist who perpetuates him. He is the two-way mirror, in which the novelist sees both himself and society outside. It occasionally happens that the novelist, busy with literary theories, or fighting those who would dictate them to him, cannot always give the picaresque hero the fictional and philosophical honour he deserves. But the novelist neglects him at his cost, because the picaresque hero, more than any other, gives an accurate picture of the world in which he operates.

By his antics, adventures and observations, and by his fate, which is specific to that age, the eternal Guzman takes society most ruthlessly and entertainingly to pieces, for the edification and delectation of all.

Some time in the 1960s I read *Guzman de Alfarache* (1559) by Mateo Aleman, *Lazarillo do Tormes* (1553) by – as far as we know – Diego Hurtado Mendoza, and *El Buscon* by Franscisco de Quevedo. Such an enjoyable experience gave me the idea of writing a picaresque novel set in modern-day England.

The picaresque novel came from Spain of the *Siglio de Oro*, and led through France to England, taking a firm hold among its writers. Where the Armada failed, literature succeeded – as it always does. Writers subsequently influenced included Defoe, Fielding, and Tobias Smollett. Sir Walter Scott later claimed to be a devotee of Alain le Sage, who wrote *Gil Blas,* translated by Smollett. Le Sage, however, was a Frenchman.

In August 1804 Henri Beyle – the great Stendhal – advised his sister Pauline to read *Gil Blas,* thinking that from his books she would learn something about the ways of the world.

How much wiser if he had told her to begin with Mateo Aleman. But at least Le Sage's picaresque novels were to influence Stendhal, in the writing of *Le Rouge et le Noir,* and *La Chartreuse de Parme.*

For over a year – and a very enjoyable time it was – I entertained myself, as much as I hoped to amuse any future readers, by writing a novel called *A Start in Life.* As to what it was about, I quote the publisher's blurb – since I wrote it myself:

'*A Start in Life* describes the ordinary and not so ordinary adventures of a bastard and a proletarian to boot, of his birth and youth in his native city, and of what befalls him when the star of his destiny takes him to London and sundry places beyond. It tells of his infamous follies and foolish mistakes, of how they led to an ending which should surprise no one, but which will not be revealed until you get there.'

The hero, Michael Cullen, after many adventures, and a term in prison for gold smuggling, was left at an appropriate end. But a picaro never dies, at least in the mind of his author. My hero nagged me to take him up again, even if only to increase the breadth of his experience.

It is comparatively easy to embark on a novel, but very difficult to know in what state of finality to leave the main character, before writing – with relief and satisfaction (those two magical words) 'The End' on the last page. The definitive ending would be if everybody died – or nearly everybody – but an author must avoid such self-indulgence or malice, tempted though he too often is.

Nevertheless, a character who had been very real for several hundred pages, and a year or two in the writing, might not be at all satisfied with his (or her) circumstances at the end of a novel: 'Why did you leave me in that situation at the end of *A Start in*

Life? I served you faithfully for 351 pages, and you left me living in an abandoned railway station with a wife and three kids. Get me out of here, for God's sake!'

What should I do? Almost immediately after the novel was published, in 1970, I began filling a notebook, describing perils and pitfalls I could put my dissatisfied hero through, and weaving them into a narrative. But other novels were being even more demanding, and fifteen years had to go by until the notebook was full enough for me to think once more about Michael Cullen, and release him from his servitude.

All picaros have a particularly engaging nature – when not being cruel, selfish, and downright criminal, as much as or even more so than the writer who gives in to the indulgence and often pleasure of describing him.

So I was impelled into writing a sequel to *A Start in Life*, with its title of *Life Goes On*. This second novel involving Michael Cullen was translated into Spanish, and published as *La Vida Continua*. At least one of my chickens came home to roost!

Even then, I could not leave my hero alone – or he could not leave me alone. I left him in a somewhat better state, though in an equally ambiguous condition, than at the end of *A Start in Life*.

After finishing *Life Goes On* I again began keeping a notebook, whose content suggested still further adventures for him, although rather more than fifteen years have since gone by – an author hopes he is going to live forever. I am these days tinkering with early chapters of volume three.

If, or when, the trilogy is complete, the ups and downs of Michael Cullen's existence will have been displayed in over a thousand pages, at which point, however, I will leave him, in an elevated station for which all his adventures have prepared him, and to which, I hope, he can have no objection. I don't, after all, want to be pestered by him for the rest of my life.

One of Joseph Conrad's characters in *Lord Jim* – I forget who it was – remarks: 'Man is amazing, but he is not a masterpiece.' The picaresque hero goes from one shady incident or daring exploit to another, as if striving to become exactly that – a masterpiece in the art of living, a complete depiction of glorious life itself, which almost from birth he had half-consciously believed himself able to attain.

If he doesn't finally appear to be anywhere near that masterpiece of the art of living then only the writer can be held responsible, because he being all-powerful created the picaro as much as the picaro created himself. The picaresque hero was the template on which the art of the writer was practised – or attempted.

The writer himself couldn't, of course, be the masterpiece Conrad was alluding to. That would be an impossibility, because anyone who becomes a writer is flawed from the beginning – though he may at least endeavour to make one out of his hero. Whether or not he fails is only for the reader to say.

The writer and the picaro are different, but they are bound up together in society, though both may well dislike the fact. I confess that two very different careers were open to me in my youth. One was to become a criminal, and the other to be a writer. How much luckier mankind is that I became a writer is not for me to say, but having viewed the alternative around me in childhood gave some insight into the workings of the picaresque mind – the mind of the picaro, that is.

The fact that both picaro and writer are so firmly embedded in society makes the symbiosis complete. A writer, by creating his own idiosyncratic picaro, proves that all picaros are unique. It is the world that is the same, both picaro and writer united by its social framework.

During his Herculean endeavours the writer portrays himself as his own picaresque hero, but because he writes instead of lives, he suffers no peril by his temerity. He used his imagination, he observes, he remembers. The landscape is his, as are the people in it, and his occupation is to write about them rather than harm them. If he does harm them, in the way of morals, it is only on paper, which they can take or leave as they wish. Nevertheless, he does not forget that he is the god who controls, who amuses himself by fabricating adventures, and thereby instructing and entertaining his readers.

Society and the picaresque hero are bound together, then, and the writer tells the story that is essential for both. Writing about the picaro may cause less harm to society than the immoral exploitations of the picaro himself but, all the same, it would be a pity of cosmic proportions if the picaresque hero ever faded from literature.

And if the same fate overtook writers, who breathe life and fire into his image, why, that would be even worse.

27 November 2002

Delacroix's Liberty

A picture I never tire of looking at in the Louvre is Delacroix's *Liberty Guiding the People*. Whenever in Paris I always go to make sure it's still there, like calling on an ancient but eccentric uncle in an old people's home, whose fascinating half-truths are so memorable one can never resist hearing more.

The painting, as everyone knows, shows a topless beauty holding a banner high and who, with a musket and fixed bayonet in the other hand, is about to advance over a heap of corpses against whatever forces are trying to suppress the uprising. People are coming up behind, in attitudes determined and hopeful, yet knowing that they too have a good chance of turning into corpses if they continue to follow her. A few may eventually take advantage of the freedom that could be gained, but the many who have stayed in safety will soon get rid of those survivors who did all the fighting.

The bearded man to the right of the Liberty wears a top hat, and carries a musket in a way that shows some military training, or experience as a hunter on his father's estates. As for Liberty herself, she may have been a seamstress, thrust forward by destiny, who in an inspired (or intoxicated) moment pulled off her chemise to give the world a sight of her bosom, on the understanding that they acknowledge her as their leader, and do not disappoint her ardent purpose.

The emphasis of the tableau is on the power pushing from behind, irresistible to those in front, and not on the emptiness that lies ahead. The romantic scene is better to look at than take part in, because the compelling notion arises that Liberty acquired through blood – if gained at all – lasts only as long as it takes those who did not fight to come to the fore and start killing those who did. Not to believe so is to be taken in by the painting's message. Scepticism is felt as keenly as the loss of innocence.

To the left of Liberty a Gavroche-like boy brandishes one of his two pistols, and one can easily imagine that he ended with both legs blown off by a cannon shot, and occupied himself for the rest of his life by selling postcards to foreign tourists outside the Louvre. Perhaps the scene, and indeed the whole painting, inspired Victor Hugo when he came to write certain chapters of *Les Misérables* a few years later.

The boy, later grown grey from suffering, eternally mal-contented, could reflect that no one who had just been inside to see the great painting would know who he was. Nor could he be aware that his hour of so-called glory (which it certainly felt to him) was continually gawped at by those who would never comprehend the misery that had driven him as a boy to pick up the pistols and follow Liberty, his elder sister, who was killed by the same ferocious grapeshot that took off his legs.

Only Delacroix the artist gained from the tragedy, and in the longer terms of human history, that must surely be right.

The Horse of Gericault

Gericault's *A Horse Frightened by Lightning* shows the perfect quadruped, noble, of harmonious proportions, and terrified, a beast for which Joseph in the Bible would have given the Egyptians much bread, or Solomon paid the going rate of fifty shekels. The longer I look at the landscape and weather, the larger the horse becomes. In a vacuum of charged air the faint shiver of equine limbs, made for strength and speed, sense an ordeal to come.

The malevolent colours of the surrounding storm, with a sandwich-thin band on the horizon pale between the earth and blue-dark sky, is in reality a few hundred feet of turbulent rain, but the fist of Jehovah is about to disperse the atmosphere into anarchy. The noble horse will no longer be a servant of Man or God, should a bolt of lightning explode like shrapnel on the battlefield and pierce those harmonious limbs. Incineration would make it offal for the kitehawks.

Four horseshoes rounded on the anvil by Tubal-Cain's descendant of a farrier were fitted to give speed over the coarse earth. Each shoe is hammered onto the hoof by handmade nails, 28 as a calendar for the waxing and waning moon.

Shoes make the horse sublime, but it feels itself a target of the gods. Lightning does not strike a shod horse, so my farrier grandfather would say, during the fiercest storm, holding a bunch of steel cutlery out of the cottage window to prove to his apprehensive wife within that there was no danger from lightning. Nevertheless, the horse cannot be sure of such immunity.

When in a state of fear, the body relates to that which makes it afraid, a connection creating the mechanism to survive. Gericault's horse is about to rear head and front legs to defy the weapons of the storm. The sheen of nervousness over its flank is manifested more in the eye, a pin-sized shine of incipient panic which even the bravest feel, and without which there is no hope of self-preservation.

The depiction of that single eye enabled Gericault to pour all his genius into the painting of his masterpiece *The Raft of the Medusa*.

1991–28 September 2000

Berlioz and the
Symphonie Fantastique

Constructive daylight dreaming, or fantasy, is the bedrock of a composer's being, without which no beginning of creative life is possible. Fantasy is the hidden emotional engine built into the mind of a young composer, and such is equally true for every artist. Fantasy is a means of dissecting reality.

So it must have been for Berlioz when, as a young man, he imagined and wrote his *Symphonie Fantastique*. I first heard it on taking up a pair of earphones looped to the back of my bed in an RAF hospital at the age of twenty. In the enforced inactivity of that year, music solaced my troubles and uncertainties, as if Berlioz – I hadn't previously heard of him – was articulating my anguish with a sublime set piece meant for me alone.

I had, after two years on active yet carefree service in Malaya, been diagnosed as having tuberculosis. Alas! Fate with hobnailed boots and a capital F slammed the door shut on a future I had set for myself.

On hearing the *Symphonie Fantastique* I became as much in thrall to the music as I was, at that age, engrossed with myself, with life and death, and all those other matters a young man must face. The music, illustrating such turmoil perfectly, came out of a genius who turned anguish into art. The significance to me was vital and immediate, in those uncertain months of thinking I could become a writer.

The work of a great artist belongs to everyone, and Berlioz, no doubt realising that his symphony not only illuminated much that was fundamental in his own spirit, knew that it would be understood by those with similar feelings. Hearing the music these days I can't fail to recall the first sense of revelation, at a time when I saw the possibility of an utterly different life to the one lived so far.

If I were to ask why his symphony made such an impression the answer would be that Berlioz's first large work was an attempt to find out who he was, to define the meaning of his life, and to ask whether it was worthwhile to go on living. This positive response to all uncertainties confirmed in his own mind that he was a great composer, and my hearing it encouraged the belief that I could recover from my illness and live the life of my choice to the full.

Much that Berlioz would subsequently write grew out of that triumphant beginning. Greater works were produced, but though all of them were enjoyable and inspiring, none were to have the same significance for him, and give me such pleasure, as the *Symphonie Fantastique*.

Speech for De Montfort University

Ladies and gentlemen, my being here today is something of a miracle, and by way of thanking you for the honour conferred on me, I hope you will allow me to explain what I mean.

Though I had little enough formal education, the prospect of continuing it for as long as possible interested me from a very early age. The getting of knowledge seemed to offer a way of understanding the world, and at the same time protecting myself from it.

I was taught to read and write as an infant, skills which led to my appearance here. Even at the Nottingham Junior Boys' School spelling and grammar were considered important, the teacher becoming a demon if one faltered over a clause or letter. One learned English, arithmetic, history and geography. Maps opened windows onto other countries, and showed them in relation to each other. The passion for self-improvement was born out of curiosity.

I read my first book, a novel, in my grandmother's house, one of many Sunday school prizes neglected by her eight children, who had brought them home. When I was eleven my grandmother encouraged me to sit for the scholarship examination (or the eleven-plus, as it was later known) having noted my obsession with the books in her parlour. I was enthusiastic at the prospect of continuing my education beyond the age of fourteen, so as to learn French and science, and many other things.

I failed the test, and also another opportunity of taking it for Nottingham High School the following year. I was disappointed, yet reconciled myself to the fact that I was not a suitable case for the treatment of education.

Nevertheless, I made the most of my three remaining years at school before going out to work. One should pay tribute to the teachers of those days who, with Spartan resources and much unpromising human material, encouraged and instructed us to the best of their ability. They were hardworking, dedicated, sympathetic, and no doubt underpaid, but they gave me something as close to a formal education as I was ever to know, and left me well equipped to get more of it on my own. I was soon to realise that while you can be robbed of money and much else, no one can take away your education.

During the Second World War, at the same time as working in a factory, I studied subjects related to aviation, having joined the Air Training Corps. I learned meteorology, English, navigation and engines – a generally scientific syllabus, which became a kind of secondary education. This enabled me to pass an aircrew selection board to train as a pilot, to get a job as an air-traffic control assistant, and then to go into the Royal Air Force and, after 28 weeks in a classroom, qualify as a wireless operator.

Back from two years in Malaya I spent a year recovering from tuberculosis, and during the incarceration kept myself sane by reading. At the same time I started to write. In the next five years I read most of what was important in world literature, that is to say, all the translations of the Latin and Greek classics. I read the prize Bible given to me at school from beginning to end, as well as Shakespeare for the first time. Convinced by then that I was going to become a writer, I read everything so as to make sure I had models to aim for.

I went to live in France and then Spain on my pension from the RAF, and stayed so long that before the age of thirty I had spent eight years out of the country. In the process I learned French and Spanish, familiarity with other languages being a great help in understanding my own.

The consequence of having had no formal education, and then after ten years being recognised as a writer, was that I had neither awe nor respect for any social organisation which sought to remain unquestioned and unchanged. Honours meant nothing except those of books being published.

A streak of anarchy, bordering on nihilism, never allowed me to take the props and integuments of social life too seriously, something which may have had something to do with the circumstances of my early life.

The role of artist, if one must be foistered on him, is to question everything, and to leave his readers at the end of the story asking questions rather than basking in the seeming certainty of answers.

One can only be inspired to create something if the mind is as free as an ever-swinging compass needle floating in a vacuum of pure spirit, yet sure in its guidance.

The artist is an individual, idiosyncratic, bloody-minded if you will, someone who sees every attempt to classify him as a threat to his power as a critic and observer. At the same time he is influenced only by that morality which civilisation has instilled almost without him knowing, and which should suffice to keep his work within the bounds of human values.

I never felt aggrieved at not having found a road into further education as a youth, though the possibility of getting some form of higher instruction would have been welcome. At an institution such as this it would have been put to good use, you can be sure, but having failed to find that alternative, by entering the system from the bottom – as it were – I have finally come through the roof! The award of an honorary degree by De Montfort University is something I shall always appreciate, as who would not? It is as important to me as the education that did not finally slip through my fingers.

Maps and the Great War

When my brain becomes stultified, as far as writing is concerned, I sometimes make for the nearest motorway to get out of London, and go on a three-day tour of secondhand bookshops. In any small country town I know which ones to look for, or think I do, though not what sort of book or books I want. Such shops vary from the ill-organised to those with rows of rigorously classified leather-bound tomes locked in glass-fronted bookcases. Familiar with both kinds, I spend more time in the former and more usual type, among mouldering novels and mildewed paperbacks, and going through the overspilling of what used to be called 'penny boxes'.

Long a haunter of such places, I know that it costs little to acquire a small library. Diligent searching turns up novels at modest prices: as a child I could go into a bookshop with sixpence and walk out with *Ivanhoe* in one hand and *Nicholas Nickleby* in the other.

Education comes from reading; the rest is instruction and experience. My enthusiasm for secondhand bookshops is undiminished, and the first question in a strange town is whether or not it is civilised enough to have one, from which people can make up a small library, read with pleasure, and gain wisdom. It is gratifying to see those of all ages sorting through the outside shelves and bins, or fascinated by the well-dressed window. England, more than any other country, is not only the Land of Book, but the Land of the Secondhand Book. My own browsing invariably turns up something I didn't know I wanted but which, once read, becomes another esoteric volume for my shelf.

I also look under tables for cardboard boxes of often out-of-date and dilapidated maps (most shops have them) hoping to find one showing the topography of a faraway and unfamiliar part of the world. I once paid a shilling for a map that had much of the left-hand side neatly cut away so as not to show the landscape and trenches behind the British line in France during the First World War (or Great War, as we knew it as children) in case it was captured during an attack – as if the Germans did not already know from aerial observation what was there.

It was a trench map, and linen-backed, in such good condition that it could not have been carried 'over the top' on 1 July, at the start of the Somme offensive in 1916. The title was: *Fonquevillers, Second Edition, 57D N.E. Sheets 1 & 2. 1:10,000.* As a military map of the Great War it had an interest beyond that of ordinary topographic maps, being a necessary accompaniment to life and death activity – and a serendipitous acquisition, since it led to the writing of a book.

All topographic maps are military in origin, in that army engineers are responsible for making them, but they also depict normal land of everyday life, from which the eye can interpret natural features, envisage man-made constructions, and imagine some drama unfolding among people who live there. A single one-inch sheet of the Ordnance Survey gives enough permutations of possible mayhem to suggest – on one level – what novels and stories a writer will concoct in a lifetime.

A military map often represents a 'theatre', to go with the resolution of those grand issues in which many thousands are killed or wounded, in comparison to the novelist's one or two casualties who perish by murder or accident – unless you happen to be writing *War and Peace.*

Fascination with maps and military history began in my early days at school. Pages from an atlas came first, then old Michelin motoring maps of France (on cloth, and dissected) at scales that suggested I might see in more detail the place where I lived. Until then it seemed I was not part of society, had neither dignity nor importance if unable to point with my finger and say: 'That's where I am.'

Pennies were also used to buy lead soldiers. Empty Woodbine packets made ideal parapets, their green a camouflage to hide defenders. Spent matchsticks stuck in joins of the wooden bedroom floor became skirmishers, manoeuvred in a kind of primitive chess, or an imaginary battle between the right and left sides of my brain.

A man next door had just finished twelve years in the Grenadier Guards. He was a sergeant, and young still, very smart and self-confident, not the sort to stay long in our area. He must have noted my interest in maps, for he gave me his one-inch Ordnance Survey sheet of the Aldershot Command, on which coloured pencils indicated tactical exercises. Recalled to the colours in 1939, it is easy to see him as a commissioned officer before the war ended.

I opened and closed that generous gift till it almost fell to pieces, but by then I knew that an inch on the map indicated 63,360 inches on the ground, a representative fraction from which could be deduced, by long division, the scale of any other map. When the schoolteacher asked how many inches there were in a mile – a hopeless question, he might have thought – I spoke out that esoteric five-figure group, to his surprise and my satisfaction.

My grandparents' cottage on Lord Middleton's estate came up for sale, and there was talk of buying it rather than continuing to rent. They had obtained a map surrounding the property or, rather, a cadastral plan to the scale of 1:2,500, from the land agents' office, and when I was eleven my grandmother, knowing my obsession, persuaded my grandfather to let me have it.

Unfolding the thin sheet showed the land I rambled on almost daily in such detail that a hundred paces covered nearly an inch and a half on the map. With pencil and rubber I arranged the units of an imaginary army in defensive positions around the group of cottages, putting them on a bridge, in a wood, along a line of railway. Infantry manned trenches in the fields. I set out machine guns for crossfire, laid barbed wire and placed my cannon.

A more solid foundation for such expertise came on finding in the local bookshop various manuals dealing with tactics and street fighting, for use by the Home Guard during the Second World War. In my passion for things military I imbibed all the information in them. After starting work at fourteen, by which time the war had been on more than three years, I went to enlist in the Home Guard, but was told by the amused captain that I was too young. In the previous war I would have been asked to come back in an hour and claim to be eighteen, and no doubt killed a few months later.

From the beginning of the Second World War to the end I listened every day to the wireless, for news from the various battlefronts. Maps of sufficient scale to follow the fighting were hard to find, only the coloured but rather schematic maps published by various newspapers being available. Wanting a map of the Stalingrad area, I sent a postal order for two shillings to Stanford's in London, and got by return a cardboard tube containing the 1:1,000,000 sheet of the area on the Volga showing the town of Tsaritsin. I still have the map, which must have been printed in about 1919. Impossible to know that 25 years later I would be walking around the battlefield in Volgograd, which in the 1990s would go back to being Tsaritsin.

At thirteen I bought the War Office manual *Notes on Map Reading*, from which one learned about intervisibility, magnetic variation, and how to find true north from the sun or stars. A map extract on a scale of 1:20,000, gridded according to the metric system, and contoured at five-metre intervals, was similar to the format of trench maps.

In childhood I heard my father and uncles talking about the Great War, and on asking my grandmother who had won it, she answered tersely that nobody had. Talk in the family concerned the dreadfulness of the conflict that seemed to have ended not too long ago. My grandmother had taken in Belgian refugees, and my blacksmith grandfather later preferred to go without meat rather than eat horseflesh. Their eldest son had been killed with the South Nottinghamshire Hussars, and an uncle on my father's side was taken prisoner on the Somme, to be mentally ill ever after. Of his brothers two had been in the army, but another had suffered as a conscientious objector. One heard talk of rationing, and Zeppelin raids. Armistice Day at school and in the town was taken seriously. When I showed the Michelin map to my teacher, he said he had used them as a driver in France during the war. Another teacher with a steel plate instead of a shoulder blade under his jacket described how he had made a barricade of dead Indian soldiers as cover for firing at the enemy.

The shadow of the Great War at times darkened our gloom, as did the rise of Hitler and Mussolini, but after September 1939 the new war was totally preoccupying, though when I joined a cadet force our marching songs were always those of the previous war.

In 1949, in an RAF hospital, I read *From Bapaume to Paschendaele* by Philip Gibbs, and realised a little more of what the Great War had been like, though Gibbs's sanitised account needed to be reinforced by the imagination, because one knew that the great trench battles of the Western Front had been misery for millions, an Armageddon for the soul of Man, a senseless demolition of the psyche.

Between 1949 and 1970 my reading of military history took in works by Sir Edward Creasey, J F C Fuller, Lidell Hart, and many others, as well as manuals on strategy and tactics by Sun Tzu, Vegetius, Clasewitz, Jomini, etc. To know what the Great War had been like, there being no one left in the family to ask, one had to read Robert Graves, Siegfried Sassoon, Edmund Blunden and Henry Williamson.

Living in a flat in West London, in the early 1960s, I went down one morning to put our daily rubbish into the dustbin, and found a pile of army notebooks that turned out to be the complete Western Front diaries of a young Canadian officer of engineers, a meticulously kept record of his experiences up to 1919 – later given to the Imperial War Museum.

Having bought the trench map already referred to, I went on to buy many others, getting them cheaply from secondhand bookshops, till my collection amounted to several hundred sheets. They were on cloth, and folded so as to fit into the tunic pocket, confirming for me that the soldiers of the British Army had at least fought, and too often died, on the best quality maps.

Beautiful layered maps accompanied the text of the *Official History of Military Operations, France and Belgium*, by Brigadier-General Edmonds, and I accumulated a complete set of about thirty volumes of this work for not very much money over the years. I also bought regimental and divisional histories, now found only in specialists' catalogues at high prices. These enabled me to learn about those terrible battles fought in mud or fine weather (though more often in mud, it seemed) of that ghastly war.

Letters and numbers on a gridded trench map make an easy system for reporting progress in the attack, but they were also used for artillery registration, this latter highlighting the fact that exploding shells accounted for far more deaths and wounds than the – shall we say? – humble bullet. One peers closely at maps for evidence of 'dead ground', and for prominences (usually in German hands), woods (cut half-way through by the contending forces) and farms (more often than not obliterated, unless there is a cellar to fortify). If an 'engagement' took place there, the interest is historical and awe-inspiring.

In the Ypres Salient trenches, lanes, houses and woods are all given English names, in a landscape where, one learned, certain features existed only as indicated by a rough post stuck near a hole of muddy water, or nailed to the stump of what had once been the middle of a wood. To match the map with the ground demands some help from the imagination. Even my few original aerial photographs make the pinpoints difficult to identify, being mostly a rash of craters and zig-zag trenches.

After twenty years of reading and research I wrote *Raw Material*, a memoir-novel whose theme was the spiritual devastation of two families by the Great War. Even so, the cemeteries and battlefields of north-east France still draw me, following maps of the time carried in plastic cases to preserve them from rain and, if I walk or cycle, from sweat. Such 1:20,000 maps of the war are more interesting – and heart-breaking – than any other maps. Individual trenches are sometimes given the names of prominent London thoroughfares, no doubt for easy identification, and to make the troops feel at home. The volunteers and later conscripts who fought and died in such countryside were the last fine human products of an era which, for better or worse, has long since gone. No other war marked such a social watershed, or left behind such a plethora of poignant memories.

The Imperial War Museum was to bring out reprints of trench maps covering the most important battle areas of the Western Front. As well as stimulating students of military history, and augmenting interest in the Great War, they are excellent for use on visits to the actual terrain. In any case, the area from the Belgian coast southwards, and into France just beyond Amiens, is well worth exploring from the tourists' point of view.

An atlas of trench map extracts, compiled by Peter Chasseaud, and called *The Topography of Armageddon*, is a publication that deals with the whole of the Western Front, and gives much information about the cartography of that war. It is an invaluable book to have in the car, or on the shelf, and should be consulted, together with other works on the subject by the same assiduous author. Collectors and anyone as fascinated by the period as myself will find it invaluable.

Secondhand bookshops are hunting grounds for all kinds of literary and cartographical ephemera but, alas, they are slowly disappearing from town centres and being displaced by shops more able to meet the rents of such prime sites – another instance of things not being as good as they were.

Government Forms

Whenever anyone starts talking about The Brotherhood of Man I want to take to the hills, with a Short Lee Enfield .303 rifle, a good stock of ammunition, and a backpack of tobacco. A bout of guerrilla warfare seems the only answer to such sentiments.

A similar amount of adrenalin thickens my blood when a government form drops through the letterbox. Other kinds of incipient injustice stir my emotions into an equal state of boil, but they may be a little more abstract and somewhat harder to rationalise. The sight of a government questionnaire, whether for income tax, a television licence, a motoring fee – but especially a census form – sends my hand feeling around the odd corners of my room for the, as yet, non-existent means of retaliation.

I suppose it's impossible to live on this crowded island without forms of some kind. So people tell me. I find it hard to believe. If somebody has to collect tax money for schools or roads or hospitals or rubbish disposal I'm willing to part with my share of the cash. Rather than go through the rage of trying to make out how all those difficult questions are to be answered, I would prefer it if the organisers of such necessary social services pushed a wheelbarrow up to my door and asked me to drop the requisite percentage of income into it. Perhaps I'd even chat with them, make jokes and offer cigarettes. But a form that demands to be filled in or else (a) I get fined or (b) I get sent to prison, is another matter altogether.

Whenever a form came through his door, my father, being unable to read or write, smiled benignly and dropped it into the fire without even wanting to know what it was about, proving that curiosity was a privilege of those who'd at least had a little education. He acted from a position of confidence because, being penniless, 'they' couldn't very well fine him. And being out of work it would be no hardship going to prison because they would then have to feed him, and provide for a family while he was away. Because of this uncompromising attitude no one ever reproached him for 'not cooperating with the authorities'.

Perhaps this was the character trait of a family whose members were born in times when forms were not nearly so prevalent as they are today. When forms did begin to drop through the box you either burned them or took to the hills. My family burned them and hoped for the best, because the fireplace was warmer than the great outside.

I suppose that as literacy gradually raised its head, people began to take a bit more notice of forms, especially if it meant the benefits of a pension book, or a certain amount of social security, or free spectacles, or an allowance of baby food.

They found that one is occasionally constrained to fill them in because one wants something. If that, as we are told, is the only way to get whatever is going, then out comes the pen and in goes the completed paper. By and large the feeling of being threatened never left them, and they always approached forms with the suspicion that they were a menace if not handled properly – or appropriately mishandled.

Some of these attitudes filtered through to me, though why they did is a mystery, since the physical act of writing comes that much easier. But even though I can write I dislike being told what to write, and threatened if I don't answer questions correctly. My reaction is to stand up against it, and the usual feelings of murder and mayhem doubled and quadrupled when, in April 1971, someone knocked at my door and handed me a census form, saying they would call back for it the following day. So would I please fill it in and have it ready?

I had always understood a census to be a simple counting of heads, and as such it would be a simple matter to complete the form. Because this one contained up to eighty questions, and if answered by all four people in the house would call for over three hundred answers, I looked on it as the form to end all forms – though I may be wrong – feeling that less intellectual effort would be involved in writing a novel than dealing with this one.

My eyes became glazed when I spread the several large sheets of paper on my desk and it occurred to me that I could not understand forms at all. Some people are number blind, and others are colour blind. I happen to be questionnaire blind. Apart from this congenital malaise I did not see what right a government office had to demand such answers from anyone. The threat of a £50 fine for not filling it in, or for telling lies, was prominently displayed on page one, as is the way with such things.

To summarise the information required would take almost the same amount of paper as was used on the form itself. And so much statistical gobbledegook that sociologists love to play around with is boring and useless to anyone with half an imagination. I decided that, since such a mountain of facts might give them softening of the brain, it would be uncivil of me to cooperate. I would act as a responsible human being for a change.

Some of the questions were sinister. If the form was answered completely it would comprise a dossier on each person. Maybe the government already has such files, I thought, and perhaps not, but if they haven't I'm not going to give information voluntarily. Let them spend a lot more on research and technological snooping devices to get it themselves, if they think it so vital to have.

To rob a citizen of anonymity is to take away his or her freedom in these days of too much bureaucracy, which is exactly what this census form was trying to do. Such callous statisticians with the blunderbuss of the law behind them are a threat to everyone.

They wanted to know not only where I was born but where my parents were born. Even if I knew I wouldn't tell them. Even if I told them I'd lie, and who can lie better than a novelist? Not that this was so important to me, but it might be of significance to other citizens of the so-called United Kingdom who happen to have come from the Commonwealth in the last few decades. If a right-wing government is ever voted into power by its honourable form-filling democratic subjects and decides to send all recently arrived immigrants back home, and they want to know where to send them, all they'll have to do is dig out the Great Census Interrogation of April 1971.

Not that I would turn down a free passage to Jamaica or Trinidad, or even Dublin (every Englishman, after all, is said to have an Irish grandmother, and I'm no exception). I've always wanted to go to Australia, in any case, but maybe many others for various reasons would not like to be so transported.

The government would get no information out of me for this particular form, short of putting a bag over my head, and blaring 'God Save the Queen' for hour after hour from loudspeakers till I could stand it no longer and was forced to give in, as is the practice, I understand, in Northern Ireland.

I handed the form back with the names of the people in the house written on it, the only addition being my own age, which I gave as 101, a not-too-subtle indication that I wasn't born yesterday – nor the day before, either.

Three hurt and puzzled officials came knocking at the door and tried to bring me to heel, but I had acted in a most civilised fashion, in that the form was not thrown into the fire as it deserves, which was progress indeed. The Authority thought otherwise, and all I had to do was sit back and wait for 'justice' to take its course.

Four months later a letter from the Registrar General asked me to reconsider my position, and fill the bloody form in or get robbed of fifty quid. Or words to that effect, except that it was written with a kind of sickly politeness more calculated to intimidate than a blatant threat. As I hadn't had an English public school and university education, such diplomatic prose was lost on me.

Nevertheless, I was tormented for nearly six months and occasionally robbed of sleep because I hadn't even had the satisfaction of seeing the form go up in flames. Violence of some sort hadn't, like justice, been seen to be done.

Everyone I spoke to said the census form was a threat to their liberty, and hated it. I did not tell them I wasn't going to fill it in. It was up to a person to do as he or she would, according to their conscience, and I didn't want to influence anybody. Not that I would have been able to, in most cases (though I wish now that I had tried) for those who made up their minds not to fill it in did so very early on, and staunchly stuck by their decision.

Sixty thousand people gave it the thumbs down, so I wasn't alone after all. It wouldn't have bothered me if I had been. I know that many of those who did fill it in lied anyway. About a thousand of us were prosecuted, the names presumably picked out of a hat.

In court at Maidstone, arraigned before three drab waxworks dead from the neck up, I called the form 'an interrogation on paper'. What annoyed the talking heads of the stuffed dummies was the untruth about my age. Such an act was holding the law of the land in contempt, so I was fined £35 with £15 costs, something I could afford to pay, though even if I couldn't, I would still not have filled in the form.

Unfortunately, the census was successful. The form-makers won. No members of parliament had objected to it, nor any organs of liberal democracy. Sixty thousand dissenters out of fifty million were too few, proving to me that the English are a nation of form-fillers. Set a form in front of somebody and he won't tear it up and throw the bits back where it came from, but reach for the pen and wonder how to fill it in so as to please and satisfy the schoolmaster or nanny hovering over him. Bureaucracy and authority can put chains on him as long as it respects his privacy while doing so. An Englishman's home is his castle, and a form to fill in lets him know his place, which gratifies him immensely. It's probably the same in any country, anyway – with, I understand, the honourable exception of Holland. When the authorities tried to perpetrate the same kind of census the freedom-loving Dutch made sure it ended in such a fiasco that it had to be called off.

Sociologists must have vast rooms packed with enough boxes of statistics to keep them going for the ten years that will elapse before another census, which will, no doubt, have twice as many questions as the one I did not fill in. I suppose they'll want to know how many times a day you go for a piss, or how often you hump a sheep, or how frequently you kick the cat.

And in that time further government forms will fall onto the heads of the form-loving populace. If they snatch out and cut them into ribbons they can make decorative paperchains. If they fill them in with a glazed look of slavish acquiescence they will make real chains around themselves impossible to escape from. The only revolution that matters is the one aimed at power and authority. Those who use power for its own ends and for its own sake, and never for the good of the people, can only be defeated by an absolute refusal to give any information whatsoever.

Politics

A few years ago I was given a flysheet put out by the University of London Union entitled: 'Alan Sillitoe and David Mercer: Traitors to the English working class'. The meeting, a talk followed by a discussion, was held on 12 November 1971: 'All progressive people welcome.' Further information on the sheet of paper said: 'A revolutionary work of literature should reflect the actual struggles of the people; emphasise the positive and best aspects of the working class; and help to build the people's confidence in their inevitable victory over oppression and exploitation. In the light of this, Sillitoe's *Saturday Night and Sunday Morning* and *The Loneliness of the Long-distance Runner*, and Mercer's *Morgan – A Suitable Case for Treatment* and *After Haggerty* are examined as examples of working-class literature. Important questions are asked: what is the attitude of each writer to the working class? How do these works of literature relate to the history of the working class? And what contribution do these writers serve? The answers are seen alongside the statements made by these authors themselves, about their aims and intentions. Considering all of these aspects, the inevitable conclusion is that these men are traitors to the English working class.'

Any reader who has come this far – for me it was no less a trial of perseverance – may wonder who could have written such dry and awful stuff. For an answer we have to be satisfied with: 'The Progressive Intellectuals' Study Group comprises a group of serious people – graduates, university students, teachers, and other professional people – united to smash the already decaying super-structure of imperialism, which is growing more and more fascist in its ideology... SEEK TRUTH TO SERVE THE PEOPLE.'

This revelation of my 'treachery' came too late for me to attend the meeting, though I would not have gone to it, having decided early on never to reply to any criticism of my writings unless it concerned a point of verifiable fact. I preferred to give the fly-sheet a place on my noticeboard, where it could be read now and again with amusement, and some satisfaction as a certificate of anti-totalitarian credentials, as well as neutrality in the imaginary class war of the Progressive Intellectuals.

I never had any allegiance to the working (or any other) classes, so how could I have been a traitor? A built-in loyalty to a Talmudic morality is one thing – of which those who write such lines as the above can have no conception – but to nitpick in the infantile maze of the so-called class war like so many chimpanzees is another.

Much has always been made of 'class' in England, and for all I know it still is, but I have been neither elevated nor crippled by such a straitjacket – whether thorny or furlined. As a child I lived as much as I could in my own world, incorruptible because corrupted already by a desire to get out of the place I lived in – at any cost. The only class I knew was the one I attended at school. As I went through the years of education (such as it was, though I never complained; and it wasn't that bad, either), my intelligence and energy were devoted to learning everything that was available, enthusiastically competing with my classmates so as to be always in the highest stream. Tests were welcomed because they defined merit, and I liked competing, but perhaps above all the contest was against that part of myself which enjoyed a natural affinity with sloth, and needed to be defeated if I was to get the most out of life.

When I failed the eleven-plus I didn't regard myself as the victim of a middle-class conspiracy to keep me in my place, but went on to obtain as much as possible from the classroom – as well as from reading at home – before going out to work.

Entering the factory at fourteen I was offended at being told that, like everyone else, I must join a trades union. I argued against it, but the law of those days said I couldn't have the job unless I became a member. An individualistic factory worker, I tolerated my new life insofar as I was earning money, helping the war effort against Nazi Germany, and learning the fundamental rules of hard work. Perhaps this was the closest I came to being 'working class', though I did not feel so at the time.

After enlisting in the Royal Air Force, happy to go in of my own free will and not wait to be conscripted, I qualified in a technical trade as a wireless operator, and worked among people from all kinds of families. After four years' service I was invalided out with a pension, which enabled me to live in France and Spain, and turn into a writer, gaining access to an occupation in which one could not belong to any class at all.

The idea of class has never infringed on my sensibility, due either to an abiding respect for my own value, or because of a protective lack of perception that kept it at bay. Only in my twenties did I begin to hear the term 'working class', by which time it had no relevance.

Others who have travelled the same route may recall different experiences, especially if they encountered a few Progressive Intellectuals on the way or even – possibly – turned into one themselves. How others view you is one thing, but more important is how you see yourself. If you know you are a unique individual (and who doesn't?) then you have some chance of considering everyone else to be unique. The notion of 'class' is a degradation, whoever uses it, or hides behind it, or complains about it.

The class-obsessed Progressive Intellectuals would have it otherwise, but I had no idea who they were, nor did I want to know. In any case I had too much respect for education to believe they were intellectual in any sense at all. The distant glimmer of something called a university, which I may have seen while taking 'the scholarship' to get into a grammar school, would not have led me to becoming one of their number. Having come so far in from the periphery I would have made more of my privilege than that.

While happy to note that my writings were in no way warped by such shades of Zhdanov-approved Soviet social realism, I did wonder at possible reasons for the Progressive Intellectuals' attitude. I recalled that in 1967 I went to Moscow as a tourist, and during my stay was invited to give a lecture at the Gorky Literary Institute.

Because I wasn't a guest – as I had been on a previous occasion – my views on writing and writers could be made known. The large hall was full, and I sat between the officials of the organisation, who clearly did not expect me to say what I did. In order not to distort an account of what was said, I quote from my notebook of the time:

'I got back to the hotel at midnight after a day of talk, talk, talk. My all-embracing and enveloping theme on every occasion is that the writer must be given more freedom, that one must not believe in social realism, that as a literary concept it is a narrow one and a sham. That one must believe in style, perfect one's style to the exclusion if necessary of all social exterior forces. I said that writers and especially young writers should not only experiment with style but be free to publish their experiments. And I said that if they can't then they may have to put them away for a few years, if the worst came to the worst, and the worst continued, that is, and keep on writing and not lose heart because one day they would certainly be able to publish them. I said all this at the Gorky Institute, to the disapproval of the dean sitting beside me; but kept on, reiterating my point and returning to it. I do so to all editors, and the staffs of magazines, force the talk onto Daniel and Sinyavsky – sometimes unable to draw them – and onto the student who got three years in prison for organising a demonstration. I mention censorship, and the students' dissatisfaction with the state of it. I often try to be subtle and disguise the initial direction of my attack by being very explanatory about theatrical and cinematic censorship in England, and turning in the middle of it to an attack on all forms of censorship in all countries, and then to an attack on censorship in Russia.'

In 1970 I wrote a foreword to a book by Colin Schindler concerning the persecution by the Soviet government of Jews who wanted to leave for Israel. Shortly afterwards an article in a Russian magazine implied that I was a dupe of the Israeli government, perhaps a Zionist agent, no less – opprobrium which I took with a certain amount of flattery. About the same time the KGB accused me of luring the interpreter-minder of Anatoly Kuznetsov (author of the novel *Babi Yar*) to my house while Kuznetsov ran into the offices of the *Daily Telegraph* and 'claimed freedom'. I was innocent of this, but was glad to be regarded as the decoy for his escape from oppression, something I would have done deliberately had I been asked. From that time my name was mud to the die-hard ideologists in Russia and, I might now assume, after seeing the paper written by the Progressive Intellectuals, in this country as well.

As a result of the Kuznetsov affair the translation of *Saturday Night and Sunday Morning,* ready at last for distribution in the USSR, was pulped on orders from the KGB – or so I was informed by a Russian friend. I in no way regretted this, because the Russian translation of my third novel, *Key to the Door,* had been so cut up and bowdlerised that it was a hundred pages less and had little relation to what I had originally written.

The book was printed in an edition of two million copies, which would have made me quite wealthy (for a while) if I had been paid in any kind of convertible currency, instead of receiving a few hundred roubles as a handout on a couple of trips to Russia in the early sixties.

Payment didn't seem too important, pirates and exploiters though the Russian publishers were in those days, but I had always thought the translation contained suspiciously few pages, until one day a German research student, Adelheid Fandry, of Hamburg University, made the book's rendering into Russian the subject of her thesis. She did a breakdown of all that had been left out, and sent me a copy.

The omitted matter was that which showed the hero to be no simple lover of socialism. Neither he nor his mates lived up to the ideal the Russians had in mind. Certain sections were cut because they did not sufficiently indicate that England was the inhuman capitalist scrapheap they liked their purblind readers to believe it was. In the Soviet version of the novel, my hero – if such he was by this time – didn't drink, or make love, or fight with his fellow-workers, or live in anything but amity with his family and neighbours. Introspection was frowned on and ripped out. Approval of his surroundings in any way quashed.

It was knife censorship – not deliberate distortion or actual re-writing, but judicious hacking, so that the finished work was nothing like the one I had written with so much care, but one of which the Progressive Intellectuals would have approved. The censors, concerned that the book contain nothing emotionally or politically disturbing, distorted it beyond recognition. Many works translated from writers in the West went through a similar mincing machine. The only consolation was that if the Russians *had* printed a faithful translation I would certainly have needed to worry about the state of my soul. In those days the only good writing in Russia came out of prison camps.

It is more than possible that some of the Progressive Intellectuals from the sixties and seventies – of warped intelligence, wilful opinions, and childish intolerance – are now in positions of power in the media or the universities. They matured, if that is the word, in the era of the slogan, of the facile reasoning in *The Little Red Book*, which was written for Chinese peasants emerging from millennia of illiteracy and ignorance, a publication that our Progressive Intellectuals nevertheless regarded as the acme of utopian philosophy.

If they didn't believe in the book themselves (though there is no evidence for this) they pushed its simplistic tenets onto others, urging them to destroy a system that had given them an education they clearly did not deserve, a system to be replaced by a state in which they would dispense 'education' of a standard low enough not to threaten their own pitiful ignorance. Their reasoning reinforced my long-held view that such socialism as they purveyed was nothing but a confidence trick of the better off to keep the workers in their place. The disaffected of that group wanted to instill into the working people (or anyone who would listen) the idea that they must not only keep their *station* but also be happy in it and adulate those so-called superiors who posed as equals in order to enslave them more securely. The workers, however, from indifference, or because of their inborn humour, or out of genuine pride and wisdom – or even bloody-mindedness – would have nothing to do with the peddling of such exhortations.

As amateur politicians, the Progressive Intellectuals could only play their game if they thought of the billions of human beings on earth as other than individuals. Politicians deal in groups, categories, or 'classes', and as soon as they get carried away by the heady game of power, think that history and circumstance can be bent to their will, and treat the individual with cynicism and contempt. People are then at the mercy of the kind of Leninist brutality that says it is impossible to make an omelette without breaking eggs. Substitute eggs for heads and the first person to get his head bashed in after a revolution is the writer, whether or not he himself wanted the revolution – more especially if he did.

As soon as my idealistic brand of social democracy fell into the hands of people who condemned me (and of course countless others) for treachery against something that did not exist, I knew that I would be among those – not only writers – who would go to the wall as soon as such Progressive Intellectuals came to power. Who but a masochist could believe in a revolution like that?

All revolutions, and the civil wars that inevitably follow, kill far more people than any Progressive Intellectual thought he was trying to save, so that in the ensuing draconian order the moral integrity of everyone is killed off as well.

Coalminers: Everything to Lose

A stretch of impeccable motorway takes me out of London through the rolling bucolic landscape of the Home Counties. Chocolate-box farms and cottages are visible here and there, as well as the occasional pocket of hi-tech well-endowed light industry. On the Great North Road, two-lane all the way, there is such heavy traffic that you wonder (if England is in the declining state it is said by all to be) whether the vehicles aren't 'Potemkin' lorries – empty, but paid for by the government to drive up and down this arterial highway to persuade people, or potential foreign investors, that business is booming. Maybe each one carries a single packet of biscuits to salve the driver's conscience.

After a hundred miles I fork left through the pork-pie-and-cheese country of Melton Mowbray, and from the highest point of the Leicestershire Wolds see – at least on a day of good visibility, which is rare – the Trent Valley and the city of Nottingham. I continue north through Sherwood Forest, the haunt of the legendary Robin Hood, who was said to rob the rich and give to the poor.

Birches, oaks, pines and firs are still blackish green from the winter. The area has a scattering of imposing ducal residences, built and maintained from the profits of timber agriculture, most of them landscaped in such a way that their aristocratic owners would not see the coalmines on which much of their wealth came to depend.

Some mines are working, others not, and crossing into Yorkshire I turn west from Doncaster through a countryside of rainswept fields. The neat stone-built village of Hickleton has one of the finest churches in the county. Driving slowly behind an enormous lorry laden with coal, I notice a stray dog in a field nosing into a sodden mattress.

Beyond a few rows of tidy houses lies Houghton Main Colliery, and by the large asphalted area of the all-but-empty car park is the settlement of the mine itself: old wheel-type headstocks (a favourite image of the cameraman when they're turning), a gridded tower with a purple, unblinking light at the top, a tall brick chimney, and various outbuildings, from one of which comes the even hum of a generator.

On the edge of the car park by the road are two temporary huts, and a caravan plastered with posters saying SAVE OUR PITS and VOTE YES FOR THE STRIKE – marking the site of the Women's Pit Camp. People sit on wooden benches by the large brazier fire, dense yellow and grey smoke moiling away on the leeward side. Overhead, a peephole of sun shows weakly through a cover of thin cloud.

One of the three young women sitting there to get some warmth offers me a cup of coffee and goes into the caravan to make it. Another woman has a beautiful blue-eyed boy of three or four at her knees, with a head of curling golden hair. He looks in wonder at the surrounding scene, and I fetch my unopened litre bottle of pure orange juice and a packet of chocolate biscuits from the car for his delectation.

Houghton Main Colliery has been out of action for some time, but the men tell me that if they were allowed to go back, the pit could be on full production in three weeks. Closer to the pit two portable cabins serve as offices, where the miners can find out if there are any alternative jobs in the area. As there never are, few bother to attend.

The only toilets at the camp are in one of those cabins, and for a while the Coal Board kept them locked to prevent the women going in. A couple of miners, however, went through a window and unlocked the doors. The Coal Board also threatened to bulldoze the protest camp away from the site, but the women telephoned newspapers and television stations so that there would be the maximum publicity, should this be attempted. Not wanting the whole country to witness their brutishness, the Coal Board let them stay.

I talked to a tall, spare, stern-looking woman with a well-lined face, who came from a pit village where all her family had been miners. 'That's why I get involved in these protests,' she said, her forthright tone coloured by a Yorkshire accent. 'I've six children, but they're all grown up now. In the 1985 strike I ran a soup kitchen, and went round the country begging money to give our kids something to eat. Now I make speeches to different groups. Tomorrow I'm going to talk to Huddersfield University. I was in London last week, and in Bradford last Saturday.

'The pit in our village was shut down just after the '85 strike, and then three more went. Now we've nothing in our area. There's no jobs at all, and no one has any prospects. People are getting married and living from day to day, and just hoping things are going to change for the better. Meanwhile they just exist on the dole money.

'When I left school at fifteen you could leave one job on a Friday night and get into another one by Monday morning, but young people these days, who have been brought up under a Thatcher government, don't expect a job to be automatic. They stay in bed till one o'clock, then they get up and lounge around the streets all day, and at night-time break into houses to pinch people's videos and television sets for a bit of money. There's a lot of thieving and drugs and prostitution, which there never was before.

'What can their parents do? They try. We know quite a few lads who come from good homes, and they use our youth club, but the buggers are just wrecking it, and it took us nearly four years to build it up out of donations.

'The reason why a lot of miners took redundancy payments is because they thought they could just move into another job, but it hasn't worked out that way. Since October the Coal Board has been spending thousands and thousands of pounds to let the men clock on to do "Care and Maintenance" only, while they decided what to do, and in the meantime the country is importing coal from abroad. I just don't understand it...'

Kevin, an intelligent-looking man of 35, with a bearskin of grey hair, was active in union affairs. He lived in a village with a mine half a mile away, and went to work there when he left school at fifteen because that was where his father worked. He thought he had a job for life, but they were told on 13 October last year that the mine was going to close at the end of the month. Pressure was put on the men to take redundancy, but the union encouraged them not to, because during the wait they would have a guaranteed minimum wage, and the pit might not close anyway.

'But if the worse comes to the worst,' Kevin said, 'I don't know what I shall do. I'll look around to see what there is, but being realistic, I see little work out there. In any case it's lower paid, and often part-time, and temporary. In the pit your work's relatively highly paid, and you can do overtime, so we're holding firm. At the moment the men are getting more money sent home every day than if they were working somewhere else.

'The local economy will be devastated. There are some industrial estates opening up, but they're very small, and they're mostly warehouses, and they often import their labour from the south. A few men were offered courses to become heavy goods vehicle drivers, bricklayers or carpenters, but when you've done the course you still find there are no jobs to go to, because there are plenty of unemployed in those trades already. People often go on such courses just for something to do.

'Up to the last few years there was never any crime in areas like these. The police didn't need to get involved because people policed their own communities. Up to now, even though there are a lot of burglaries, there aren't any muggings. But the increase in crime is more than the national average. Someone has broken into the cricket club building twice in the last fortnight. One morning a woman woke up to see that someone had actually stolen the concrete paving slabs of her garden path!

'We've always been good at looking after retired miners, arranging concerts or taking them on outings, but everything we've held dear and believed in is being chipped away. It's like going into the unknown. In my 23 years as a miner you build up a very close relationship with those you work with. You go out at night for a drink with the same people. If somebody's not watching out for you at work you get seriously hurt. You're dependent on each other, and it breeds comradeship. The strong look after the weak, and it's a feeling that spreads over the whole community.

'Now that's being taken away. You just can't imagine what it'll be like in another ten years in these areas. A whole way of life is changing. It's pure vindictiveness on the government's part, as if they've got it into their heads that they want to smash the miners for what happened in 1972, when our strike brought down the Heath government. But most of the people in the mines were only at school then.

'Seventeen pits have shut in the area, and the two that are left are said to be closing soon. I don't think economics comes into it at all, because our economic argument for keeping the pits open can't be defeated. It's as if the clock is winding England back, not to the 1930s, but to before the Industrial Revolution.'

The women moved away from the fire while one of the men replenished it with coal, increasing the clouds of sulphurous smoke that almost hid the caravan before angling upwards. The coal is opencast and soft, but is given free every week by an Irishman who extracts it from his own site a few miles away. He also leaves a bottle of whiskey and a £20 note with the women.

A forty-year-old crippled miner goes to sit by the fire. He is broad-bodied and long-haired, the chest of his black padded leather jacket covered as plentifully with protest badges as medals on the uniform of a Soviet admiral. People come by all day to talk for a few minutes, and give encouragement, or to make donations, and leave articles for the comfort of the women who work shifts from dawn to dusk at their pit camp.

A tall, somewhat sad-looking man with slicked-back dark hair and brown eyes, stood by the fire, a large black dog by his legs. He was 52 years old and has been redundant for four years, after spending all his working life in the pit except for two years' National Service with the army. I asked him to tell me about his typical day.

'I get up early from habit, and take the dog out for a walk. I then spend an hour with my father, who lives in a nearby bungalow. I do a bit of gardening, but also I'm involved in a voluntary youth group, which takes up quite a bit of time. Then I go to the club and have a drink. I also help to run an amateur boxing club four night a week, and try to organise outings for the kids. I've got a car to get around in, and there's plenty to do, but sometimes I get really fed up, and then I might go more often to the pub. The biggest part of the time, though, I'm occupied. I watch some television, but I'm not addicted to it. I also read quite a lot, because the local library will get you any book you want.

'My brother is in the same situation as me, and he has two big allotments, because he's a keen gardener. He also goes swimming every day, and is involved in the village tenants' association, arranging meetings, and getting a credit union organised. But not a lot of people take part in such things.

'I get unemployment benefit, and I've still got some of my redundancy money, though that doesn't last forever. A lot who took redundancy after 1985 were fifty-years-old and above. They got a lump sum of £20,000, plus x amount of pounds weekly till they were 65, then £68 index-linked state benefit. Then the Coal Board discovered how expensive this arrangement was, and only paid straight severance pay, and that was that. There were two or three different versions of redundancy, but basically that was it.

'People a bit younger than me, who took severance pay four years ago, had a good time for a couple of years, and now they're on rock bottom. No work to go to. No future at all. It's caused trouble with people's marriages. As they say, when poverty comes in by the door, love flies out of the window. There's tension in the house, and couples split up.

'The younger generation's running haywire. They've been abandoned by society. Older people are saying you ought to bring back the birch and things like that, but I don't agree. Last night at the youth club they were creating mayhem because the leader came from a different area, and they weren't showing her any respect. Me and my wife went to sort them out, because when we are there they don't perform like that. We know their parents and grandparents. A lot of the youths will be here tonight, because we've got a pop group coming from Sheffield. That'll keep 'em occupied for a couple of hours.

'Lads like that don't go on to further education. They know as well as I do, and as all their teachers know, that after the courses are finished there are no jobs for them to go to. There was a caretaker's job advertised the other week at a village school and it got 292 applicants – for one job!'

A woman by the fire told me about her stepson, who worked twelve hours a day for £80 a week – after his stoppages from £120 gross wages. 'He has three children,' she went on, 'but would rather work for such a rate than stay at home. He has to have a car to get to work, and qualifies for family supplement of £31 a week. He lives in a council house and pays a rent of £23 a week. The cost of school dinners for the children leave them with nothing to spare.'

After the closure announcement last October the miners and their wives went on well-supported marches and demonstrations. When Arthur Scargill, the miners' leader, asked the TUC for support, he was told that they don't want to go back to the bad old days of striking. But miners don't think of such militant times as the bad old days:

'I remember when I was at the pit,' another man told me, 'we had disabled persons and people with learning difficulties working alongside us, and we used to look after them, and at the end of the week we all went out together. Everybody was friendly.

'The workforce in the mines is now an average age of 32 or 33, and I don't think the future's quite sunk in, and what the end result will be. Sixty-nine per cent of the workforce is ready to take strike action, but whether we'll achieve what we want remains to be seen. We've come to the stage, though, where there's nothing to lose, not only for the miners, but for the whole country.'

The pattern of their hopes and fears becomes plain, the same half-hidden consternation on their faces kept in its place by doing all they can to make their plight known to a wider public, which includes telling the obvious truth that the miners' plight today will be that of other trades and professions tomorrow.

The sites of former collieries are being flattened and re-landscaped, some to become building plots for supermarkets and industrial estates. Going through one town I saw that the Honda Reliant shop was boarded up, as was a jewellers' next door, though such scenes aren't only evident in these areas.

Driving westerly towards Doncaster, mining settlements separated by impressive environs of semi-wooded hills, one passes Conisborough, with its spectacular ruined castle featured in *Ivanhoe*.

Forty kilometres south of Houghton Main is the village of Tibshelf, in Derbyshire, which lost all but one of its mines some years ago. I walk into the social club on the main street, and join a dozen or so men there for a drink.

A huge white platter of meat sandwiches is set on the bar for members to help themselves. A man of about forty, of medium build, with a short haircut and light-blue eyes, and neatly dressed in jacket and jeans, stands at the bar by his pint of beer. He was made redundant six years ago and, showing the traditional initiative of the intelligent few, now works as a builder on a Greek island.

He went, rather than stay at home idle, and at first he was prepared to do any kind of work there, sometimes going into the hills to help the local people at harvest time. He now makes more than a fair living with his expertise, and though occasionally feeling the isolation, is happy enough with the arrangement, which enables him to come back to Derbyshire two or three times a year to see his wife and children.

Tibshelf is within reach of such big towns as Derby and Nottingham, but there is unemployment in those places also. The

Raleigh Bicycle Company in Nottingham, which in its heyday had eight thousand workers, now needs only two thousand, while Players' tobacco and cigarette factory, which had seven thousand workers, no longer exists.

There is an industrial estate near Tibshelf, but many of the men in the village remain *dolers* – on the dole. One redundant miner, who lives at Eastwood, stays at home as a 'house-husband', doing the cleaning, cooking and looking after the children, while his wife goes out to work. Another man in the club commented that once upon a time if a miner was laid off for a while he might get work at one of the surrounding farms, but these days agriculture is too automated to need anyone. He also knows a group of local men who went to Spain with their redundancy money, but it was impossible to get work so they came back to live on the dole.

Further down the road is the 'Crown' pub, where some ex-miners are gathered at the bar. The publican himself, a tall, well-built and hearty man, had worked at the pit for 31 years. The others tell me they have now got jobs, one man saying you can always find work if you look hard enough. Another makes a living as a painter and decorator. He complained at the treatment miners receive from some British newspapers. 'They think we're all cloth-capped, whippet-fancying morons. When a reporter comes up from the South to interview somebody in the Miners' Institute all he does is talk to an eighty-year-old wearing a cloth cap, who left the mines twenty years ago and doesn't know anything about the job any more.'

I called at the one mine remaining in the area, Silver Hill, which is among those threatened with closure, after hearing the suggestion in the pub that the management were sabotaging the pit so that the men won't be able to go back, even if the government decides to keep it going. The Union Jack flies proudly from the top of a three-stage concrete structure, as if someone had started to build the Tower of Babel but left off on the understanding from God Almighty that there was no need to go any higher, provided they planted the British flag there.

A notice by the gate states that the plant is Coal Board property, and that the public should keep out. I wander around inside but there is no one to be seen, though the ancestral smell of coal is in the air, and the usual generator whines from somewhere. A row of neat houses along the lane backs on to open fields, where a solitary horse contentedly grazes at the rich grass.

Four kilometres north-east of Tibshelf stands Hardwick Hall, a sixteenth-century mansion noted for the size and number of its windows. It was built by the architects Smithson (father and son) for 'Bess of Hardwick' – the Countess of Shrewsbury. A remarkable woman, she was married four times, being left progressively richer by the death of each husband.

The hilly country roundabout is of the choicest. No coalmines can be seen, only farms on partly wooded hills that are pale and of various greens under a gentle sun, such colours suggesting a beauty and depth redolent of an England before the Industrial Revolution.

Birds of spring sing melodiously sweet and, looking into the park from the lane, one sees a lake on which two white swans are floating, their necks curved in perfect unison and alignment. Fields near the gate have been spring ploughed into a rich chocolate loam, and I go slowly through the well-cropped pastures, to the open grounds of the Hall so as not to disturb the indolently grazing long-horned cattle.

Another stately mansion, now a museum, is Wollaton Hall, a couple of miles west of Nottingham, built and paid for from the proceeds of coal pits in the sixteenth century. The cost of £80,000 was enormous for those days, but the owner, Sir Francis Willoughby, died in poverty in London.

After visiting the place for old times' sake, I sat in The Broxtowe Inn, a large, modern pub on the outskirts of Nottingham, talking to a miner who works at Cotgrave colliery, which is also under threat of being closed. He told me about his life, and possible prospects for the future.

'I was born not far from a colliery, and can remember one or two of the old miners walking along the road by our house after work. As a child I used to dream that a miner would come up one night from the depths of the earth and through the floor in the middle of our living room!

'At fifteen I left school and did an apprenticeship in plate welding at an engineering firm. After seven years I met a friend, who told me there were vacancies at Lynby Pit, and when I told my mother I was going there for a job, she said: "You're not. You're not going to work in the pit. I won't let you."

'In those days people thought you only went to a coalmine when it was impossible to get work anywhere else. My own grandfather, who wouldn't let his three sons go down the pit, worked at Wollaton Colliery as a blacksmith, shoeing ponies underground until he was seventy. He cycled there and back each day, and never had a good word to say for the place, though that was when the mines were privately owned. In those days, before welding techniques became general, blacksmiths worked at the forge, making shoes for horses, and chains out of steel, as well as fabricating chisels, hammers, or their own tools – skills which have gone forever.

'I told my mother that going down the pit would be a good job for me, and I went to see the engineer, who said: "We'd like to have you, but at the moment there are no vacancies. If you take a medical, though, in six months' time you'll probably get a job."

'When a chap rang me up and told me I could start I felt great, because I was going into a secure industry. Not long after, I decided to get married. Everything was good. I really loved the work. I loved the challenge. It wasn't like any working environment I'd ever known. At first they sent us to Hall Green to learn the techniques of working underground, self-rescue training, emergency first aid, how to pack prop supports, and working haulages.

'When the closure was announced at Lynby a lot of the men left, but then it was postponed for a year and they wished they hadn't. I went to Blidworth, five miles away, and remember sitting in the canteen debating what to do. My wife was pregnant, and I had to get settled. The manager said he could guarantee that we still had forty years of coal to get out, and I thought: "I'm 37 now, and in fifteen years that'll be me finished." I was happy. I toyed with the idea of buying a house, but couldn't find one because it was the boom time of the eighties. So I bought one nearer to Nottingham, which was the best thing I ever did, because Blidworth closed a couple of years later, and I went to work at Cotgrave.

'When I came here five years ago I didn't know anybody, but the men welcomed me with open arms, and I couldn't have wished for a better place to be. I used to make a point of having a pint at the Welfare, and when I stood at the bar the others would shout: "Oy! Come over here, mate, sit here," as if we'd known each other for years. And even outside the mine, if I said to my mates that I was in trouble, they'd all be ready to help. For me, that spirit will be one of the hardest things to leave behind.

'Our coal at the moment is the best in the area, with no sulphur in it whatever. Cotgrave doesn't need to blend its coal before selling it to the power stations. Every cobble we turn out we can sell. It's true that Cotgrave has lost three million pounds, but we'd spent a million of that opening a new face. We've got the phenomenal amount of 240 million tons of coal in reserve, and the Boyds Report recommended that we keep our shafts open, so all we can think is that if it comes to privatisation the money-men will buy the pit and make a killing, and the public will end up paying higher prices. If they'd let us get coal until March of this financial year we'd have been back in profit, but they stopped us so that they could say the pit was not viable.

'There's been no major industrial conflict in the coal industry since 1985. We've gone about our jobs and done everything that British Coal could possibly ask us to do. "You've got to produce," they say, "you've got to produce." So we did. You go mad. You get as much coal out as you can, till you're going like a robot. And then they come back to us and say: "Stop! You're producing too much. We can't sell it all. We don't want your coal any more..."

'We stood in our canteen when they announced the closure. The union got us in to tell us it would be compulsory, that there'll be no transfers to other pits, and that the redundancy scheme as we know it is non-existent. You could hear a pin drop. People looked at one another and, I'm not ashamed to say it, men had tears in their eyes. At another meeting that day we heard there was a possibility that the government would make redundancy payment, though it wasn't definite.

'The rumour going around the pits before the closure was announced last October was that there would be £10,000 for anybody over thirty, if they left before March. This was to put pressure on the men to go: you either take it now, or you'll lose everything. Some people went, and I see old mates who tell me they dropped the biggest clanger when they did, but I reminded them of all the pressure that was put on them to do so. Mentally, you've got to be able to cope with the situation, knowing you've got to make a decision, but that even so the decision you make can go against you, because you can find out that though you made it on the basis of what was happening at the time, everything can change after you've gone.

'Recently I've started looking for work outside the coal industry. I've never wanted to, because I love my job, but I've come to the decision that now is the time to get out, because no matter what they say they're going to do, or what pits they are trying to keep open, judging by what they've got rid of in the last five years they'll keep picking us off till we're left with about twelve pits in the country. Our industry's not only invaluable to us, it's invaluable to the country as well, so why don't they let us get the coal out now, and stockpile it for the future?

'They'll do everything to wipe us out, but it's not just thirty thousand miners who'll go, because with their wives it's double. And if you count dependents as well, it's a whole lot more. And that's just the coal industry. Think of all the subsidiary industries dependent on it. Belgium, I think it was, once had a thriving coal industry, but because the Germans started selling coal at a cheap rate they closed most of their mines, offering massive redundancy payments. As soon as they'd gone, the price of German coal rocketed, and Belgium then had to pay sky-high prices. It'll be the same with us. Our industry will go, we'll rely on imports, and the price will shoot up.

'Asfordby, a brand new mine a few miles away, has been developing for about fifteen years, and it's not coaling yet. The Coal Board has put good money into it, so it'll get privatised, but even if we were able to transfer there we could be out of a job in six months, because it'll be "hire and fire" as in the old days before nationalisation.

'At Cotgrave we just clock in and out, but I've heard tales – I don't know how true they are – where chaps come in at Asfordby and say: "I'm sorry I'm late, gaffer, but my car broke down," and the gaffer says: "Don't worry, because you won't be coming in any more." At Cotgrave, if you're a few minutes' late you just stay a bit extra on your shift to make up for it, but at Asfordby it's: "You start at this time, and you stop at that" – by the clock. Things don't always go like that. If you cut corners underground, you're dead. Another thing is that in a privatised coal industry you'll go into a contract situation, and there'll be no job security whatever.

'A "Job Shop" has been set up at the mine to tell us how to fill in application forms, and what else to do when we go out looking for jobs. This is supposed to give you confidence, but it only ends up diverting your attention from the problem of the pit closing.

'When one of the men came into the canteen on Monday, and told us he had found a job, the atmosphere among the rest of us was euphoric, but in the next few days everyone was quiet again, and you could see the expression on their faces saying: "I wish it was me."

'We talk about the wives getting onto us about not doing anything at home, but you don't have any incentive with all that turmoil going around in your head. I used to love coming off shift and taking the kids out. I got my body used to having six hours' sleep instead of eight so that I could have another couple of hours' leisure time. Or I would say: "Right, I'm on nights, but I'll get up at one, and redecorate the kiddies' bedroom." But now, I get home and I can't motivate myself, and in any case I'm trying to save as much money as I can because we're on a basic wage, with no bonuses now we've stopped coaling.

'My wife's mother came yesterday, and said to me: "What's the matter with you? You're quiet." "Well," I say, "perhaps I am." My wife puts her arms around me as if to say: "We're in this together." Some people go home and get no support. They're going to be out of a job, and out of a wife as well.

'I think that if I could get a five-day-a-week job with normal hours I might start living again. As it is, when the kids get a bit uppity I shout at them, and then think afterwards that in normal times I wouldn't have done. I've always believed that a man should be a breadwinner and provide shelter for his family. It might sound a bit Stone Age, but that's how I was brought up, and I don't want that taken away from me.'

Early in 1960 I was asked to write a commentary for a short film devoted to how miners spent their leisure. Karel Reisz was to be the director (he made the film of my novel *Saturday Night and Sunday Morning*) and it was his view that for such a subject we should also see something of how the miners did their work. This meant spending a day down Clipstone Pit, and going to the face from which coal was being hewn.

Even though machinery ripped out the coal, miners still worked in three-foot seams a thousand metres underground and three thousand metres distant from the lift shafts. They toiled in thick dust and semi-darkness, in conditions which seemed entirely inimical to human beings. When I got back to the surface after eight hours all I wanted to do was drink pint after pint of liquid, and I had only been observing.

Nevertheless, the miners enjoyed their leisure to the full, and lived well. At that time there was no industrial unrest, wages were probably as fair as they could be made, and no one dreamed of a time when coal would no longer be wanted. Nationalisation had been in operation for fifteen years and, at least from an outsider's point of view, the industry seemed to be working smoothly. In their spare time the miners played bowls, tended their gardens, or spent evenings chatting and drinking in the Welfare Institute. Some played in the brass band, which was almost the only music I heard during my childhood. One could never forget, at the sound of such music, that the miners' existence was hard and dangerous, and far from ideal, but all the evidence was that as a way of life it would continue.

'How do you change, though?' the Nottinghamshire miner said. 'Ninety per cent of me wants to stay where I am, while the other ten per cent tells me not to be a fool. They say we're going to know for sure on Thursday, and I go home and get on with my life. Then, when Thursday comes, they tell us we might not know till after Easter. And then after Easter it might be another fortnight after that. It's hard to keep yourself physically and mentally together when you know that at the end of it all you're going to be out of a job.

'So all the time now I'm thinking about what I'm going to do. You cry out for comfort. In a Coal Board environment I've had security for fifteen years, and some have had it for thirty or even more. We don't know any other, and to lose it is more frightening than anything.

'Wherever I go, if I leave the industry, I'm not going to be secure. If I let the redundancy money go, which is there at the moment, and move to another pit, I could be out of work with nothing in six months. I'll get a job of some kind, because after your redundancy money's gone you've got nothing. You're on the dole, and it's the wrong time of life to be on the dole.

'Some of the men have found out, now that they're fifty, that if they don't take their pension and finish before March they'll have to wait another ten years before they get it. That kind of blackmail has been going on for months, and we're getting nearer to the crunch. We're going down a tunnel that the government's planned. They'll wipe the floor with us, because of the dispute of '84. There's some talk about going on strike, but the public will turn round and say: "Here go the miners, striking again!" – and my personal belief is that it'll go against us.

'Some of the younger men took on mortgages because they've got young families, and when the closures were announced they were under pressure. Like everybody else they have credit to meet. They've been told that there'd be no compulsory redundancies, because they could be moved from pit to pit to fill the places of older men who retire. But that's not true any more.

'The redundancy payment will be the equivalent of a year's wages to us, so if you look at it that way, it's not so much. When it gets to below £8,000 and you're out of work you get some income support. The first thing people think of when they get their redundancy money, though, is to pay off their mortgage and keep a roof over their heads, but that's not allowed as a legitimate way to spend your money. You just can't do that, and then go on the dole, because they'd ask you where your money was. It kicks your legs from underneath you, and while you're down they'll chop off your arms so you can't get up again.

'A friend of mine who accepted redundancy money has just taken on some heavy debt, which is unusual for a man of fifty, but he did, and then he found out he can't get a job – after thirty years in the pit. When I saw him I asked whether he'd been applying for any jobs. "No," he said, "I just keep on spending my redundancy money. I've still got a lot of it in the bank." Afterwards I thought: "Yes, but how long will it last?"

'One of the men committed suicide, and we don't know whether it was related to the pressure he was put under. He was 36 years old, but also a big drinker, so that might have helped, but you'll never know the moral consequences of what they're doing to us. Not everybody's got a strong will, and I wonder how many people are on the brink?

'I know some whose redundancy money won't last five minutes. They say, "I'm going to have a new car, new windows and a good holiday." If you're getting £15,000, a new car costs five, windows five, a holiday three, and what are you coming back to? They're not used to having that sort of money. Soon they'll have nothing. Social Security might pick up the tab after a year, but what sort of a life is that?

'It's our pride. Take people's pride away and you leave them with nothing. I tell myself they're not going to grind me down, but it's been bloody hard work to keep that front up. I've broken down a couple of times at home, and I've been close to it at work when we get talking, but I'm not letting my pride go. They've got good tacticians on the Coal Board side, though, and they know very well what they're doing.

'The government's good at cooling the situation down. We look in the newspapers and you only get snippets now and again. People outside don't bother much about what's happening in the pits. They just turn the page over. We're hoping it'll get back in the public eye in the next few weeks. On a day when there are big articles in the press it's like going to a football match. You've scored a goal and shout: "Hooray!" You're all up in the air, wanting another one, but the match goes on and on and on, and nobody scores – no more articles – so everybody's interest dwindles.

'We don't know what type of work we're going to find when we get out there, if any. I've never known anything like it in my entire life. I want to get out, but I daren't because if I leave and find the pit doesn't shut, I'll be kicking myself. I want to get out, yet I also want to stay, but then I might find my job's gone and I *have* to get out. It's like being a condemned man looking into your grave. You're going to get thrown a rope, or you can run off and leave it.

'When I'm looking at both ends of the rope, as I am now, I don't know which one to grab. But once I know it's all finished for sure and my back's against the wall, I can come out fighting. I can say: "That's that, then." I shall rise from the ashes, because that's where my strength lies.'

One wonders what will be left of the coalfields if the present trend continues, which looks likely to be the case. Will not only the coal area but the whole country become a tourist paradise and turn into a bed-and-breakfast island, a theme park for foreign visitors? Or will England be used only as a vast recyclement centre for the world's rubbish, atomic or otherwise?

It's anyone's guess. Certainly there is no prospect that the miners will go back to what D H Lawrence in his more splenetic moments wanted: miners dancing around the greenwood tree in their gaily woven clothes, and no longer the people he feared, because they were mindless and as happy as can be. Or is England scoring another first in the history of the world by pioneering a way out of the Industrial Revolution for all other countries to follow?

It's hard to say whether the mood among the miners is one of complete despair. There is in many a kind of intelligent resignation that still provides a bedrock of hope. The latest news, however, is that all the pits mentioned in this article are doomed.

Robinson Spedding's Eight Golden Sovereigns

In 1910, a tall young man of independent spirit laid eight golden sovereigns on the counter of a shipping office in Newcastle-upon-Tyne, and bought himself a passage to Canada. His name was Robinson Spedding (always Rob for short, when he spoke to me) and he had worked from the age of fourteen in a coal mine in County Durham, and saved money shilling by shilling so as to go abroad and improve the standard of his existence. 'I must have dreamed of doing it before I was born,' he told me, when he was an old man. During the eight-day crossing he shared a cabin, and had regular meals at a dining room table. He did not, he emphasised, go steerage.

A passport wasn't necessary in those days and, after landing at Halifax Nova Scotia, work was easy to find because it was summer. He was content to labour at whatever was available, but when winter came he was laid off, and life was hard. He survived, so that in a couple of years he was, as he put it, in easy street.

At the beginning of the Great War, in August 1914, he was in Edmonton, Alberta, and immediately enlisted because 'though I could have hung back, like some, I just thought it was my duty.'

He served three years and three months with the Canadian Army in France, and fought in many hard battles, the Canadian (and Australian) divisions often being used as shock troops in the big attacks. 'I didn't get a scratch in all that time,' he said, 'because I took everything as I would in normal life. Things were rough in

71

those days, and I'd been a coalminer, don't forget, though I suppose I was lucky.'

'At a railway cutting near Hill 60 I was battalion Gas NC0, and when the Germans sent over mustard gas shells, Brigade HQ wanted a report, so I went out to investigate. Without realising, I picked up a piece of shell case, and got covered in blisters from head to foot. I was nearly blind for three weeks. I insisted on staying in the trenches, but eventually they twigged my condition and sent me back to England as a casualty. Maybe it saved my life, picking up that piece of gas shell.'

On demobilisation he married a woman from Kent, and the pair of them had long-term plans. They went to County Durham, and Rob worked two years of double shifts (sixteen hours a day) at a time when the Sankey Award gave miners good wages – for those days. He and his wife Ethel saved every penny, and when they had enough went back to Kent and rented a farm, which they eventually bought. Rob died ten years ago, in his eighties, and Ethel continued to manage the farm till she too died, in her nineties. They had given me permission to roam anywhere over their land, potting rabbits with my shotgun.

The point of this perhaps not unusual story is that Rob Spedding, when the urge came upon him as a young man, was free to leave his country and try to get from life what he knew he deserved, yet was prepared to work for. Perhaps such freedom had led him to volunteer so promptly in 1914, to come back to his country when it needed him. In other words, a free person is of more value, both to himself and everyone else, than a slave is.

Moral obligations go with freedom of movement but, 'have the fare, want to go' or, even better, 'have feet, can walk', should be unquestioned. A government that refuses the right of someone to buy a train ticket to the nearest port or frontier is intolerable and should be swept away, but in Russia today tens of thousands of Jews wishing to get out are not allowed to do so.

No doubt tens of thousands of other people in that country would also like to vote with their feet, and they too deserve support, but one can only remark on individuals, and the person

I have in mind is a frail, middle-aged woman of great courage and persistence, whose name is Ida Nudel.

On first applying to leave for Israel in 1972, to join her sister, she lost her job in economic engineering, and could only get manual work, for which she was totally unsuited. Since then she has signed collective letters calling for the right to emigrate, has taken part in strikes and demonstrations, and helped those in prison who also dared to ask for exit visas. She was repeatedly arrested and interrogated, then sent to Siberia for four years, where she lived in conditions that would daunt all but the most robust. Now banished to the town of Bendery, near the Rumanian frontier and seven hundred miles from her home in Moscow, she is ill, and still harassed by the police.

The self-reliant Geordie coalminer who put his eight golden sovereigns on the counter of the shipping office did not have to apply for an exit visa, and I know what he would have said about any government that demanded one. Nor did he mention being lucky enough to live in a country he was free to leave and come back to. Why should he?

If Ida Nudel had the equivalent of eight golden sovereigns, would she be able to get on a train to Odessa – a mere sixty miles away – and walk into a shipping office, and take the money from her handbag, and set it on the counter, and ask for a ticket to Greece so that she could then go on to Israel? Would she be issued one?

She would be the happiest person in the world, but the fact is that even if she walked to the outskirts of the town of Bendery she would be turned back. If I thought there was half a chance I would get the money for her myself, and ask her to perform the ritual of the eight golden sovereigns, but there is no question at the moment that whoever it is would allow such a thing to be done, even if only as a tribute to the memory of Rob Spedding, the Kentish farmer and one-time coalminer from County Durham.

Confessions of a
Smoking Monster

When I was fourteen my father said, from inside a cloud of nicotine smoke: 'Alan, you ought to give up cigarettes. They're not good for you. They're coffin nails.'

His amiable mood meant I could risk a response. '*You* smoke 'em, though.'

'That's because I can't help it. You should get yourself a pipe. A pipe's healthier. The streets are full of nub ends to fill 'em with.'

We've always been smokers in our family, except my two sisters, who died of cancer in their forties. At the end of my mother's life she would sit watching television with a Park Drive smouldering in one hand, and a mug of strong tea in the other.

I took to cigarettes on going to work in a factory. Smoking was probably less harmful than the reek of machine oil, metal dust and disinfectant suds that I stood in for eight hours a day.

A couple of years later I did buy a pipe, influenced by seeing them wielded by RAF aircrew, a cheerful, intelligent and heroically doomed lot. I was, in any case, training to become one of them. Whoever else smoked a pipe seemed to be enjoying it, and when I got used to the procedure of filling and igniting it – and poking and reeming – it was obvious why. The tobacco was ambrosial. A freshly opened tin smelt like Christmas pudding which, lit on a cold dark night, on my way back from a long session of love making in a girlfriend's house, filled the mouth and the air round about with a comforting and irreplaceable fragrance.

On active service in Malaya I took a fancy to the local brand of cheroot, and always had a bundle between my morse key and log book, to while away the fourteen-hour night-watch in a hut beyond the end of the airstrip. I had a pipe and pouch of tobacco, as well as a tin of Craven 'A' cigarettes ('made specially to prevent sore throats') – the weekly allowance to other ranks. Tobacco fumes kept away noxious insect life, and no doubt a snake would have turned tail at the first whiff of cheroot smoke. A nibbling mosquito would certainly have dropped dead after its drink of my blood.

The addiction was complete, and I saw no reason to live without it. Maybe you're now wanting to know how, due to a social conscience, and an inborn sense of self-preservation, I fought a noble fight and gave the habit up. If so, read no further.

On returning to England my demob X-ray showed positive signs of tuberculosis. If I had nothing to lose before, I had even less now. Strangely perhaps, no one was forbidden to smoke in the RAF hospital. Morale, as Napoleon wrote, was as three unto one, and the wise doctors must have thought so too. After a minor operation my first act on being tipped back into bed was to have a few puffs on a cheroot before going to sleep.

Demobilised and pensioned off at 21, who could say that a pensioner ought not to smoke? For nine years I had the use of only one lung, but in Majorca during the fifties tobacco was twopence an ounce, so on my pittance smoking was no problem. Even cigars were affordable now and again. You smoked, or you didn't. Most people smoked. Walking into a café was like being in the proximity of a haystack about to ignite. In winter it was comforting and warm. In summer one could sit outside.

Not long ago I woke up in the morning with unaccustomed joy in my heart on realising I was too old to die young. I could go on smoking, drinking and doing anything else of which I was capable, and to hell with it. If I died ten years before my time, what was one decade when set against the blackout of eternity?

So for more than fifty years I've smoked a pipe, though I try not to light up before ten in the morning, or less than two hours after getting out of bed. By then,

'Tobacco, tobacco,

Sing sweetly for tobacco!'

is trilling through my head, and the first pipeful has its usual intoxicating effect.

People tell me I'd be healthier if I stopped. You'll live longer. You'll save money. You won't be such a bane to others. But the real reason anti-smokers try to get at you is that they don't like seeing anybody enjoy themselves. You disturb their notions of right and wrong. You make them uncertain about their respect for law and order. An example of free will is upsetting. Everyone should be like them; they don't smoke, so you shouldn't.

There's something of an inquisitor in nearly everybody, which likes to ban, to forbid. If someone had enforced smoking during the Second World War we'd have lost. Be like me, they imply, able to enjoy life just as much as you, but without smoking. The militant anti-smoker would like to see you arrested on the street. All I say is that if ever I give up smoking, send for a doctor. No, call the undertaker.

'Ah,' exclaim the anti-smoking miseries (they won't leave you alone) 'but if you become ill as a result of your ineradicable vice, what about the cost to the National Health Service?' 'Well,' I might reply, 'what Health Service, for a start?' In any case, the smoker is unlikely to occupy more of the country's medical services than the valetudinarian anti-smoking vegetarian deliquescent, who lingers for years in his bath chair, looked after by a disgusted family, who wished he had snuffed it years ago. Apart from that, imagine dying earlier from some affliction unrelated to tobacco, as many non-smokers obviously must. What irony, that in the moments before blackout you regret all the cigars, pipes and cigarettes you hadn't smoked – alas, too late.

Those who have recently given up smoking look so forlorn they are no encouragement to whoever still smokes. Whenever I see such a person all I can do, out of pity, is to offer him (and occasionally her) a cigar. Sometimes it is accepted and, having suffered hell's torments for six months or so in the process of giving up, the poor soul sucks greedily at my humane offering, so far back in heaven it is a delight to witness. I never go to a party without a few extra cigars in my pocket, they being easier to seduce with than cigarettes or a pinch of tobacco.

Anti-smoking zealots regard such humanity as corruption. They would have me hemlocked if they could, but surely they would consider my self-indulgent wallowing in tobacco sufficient poison to save them doing the job. And since ninety-nine per cent of articles about smoking say it should be banned, they can hardly, in the land of free speech, object to the measly one per cent (if that) which extols it.

A photograph on my bookshelf shows Isambard Kingdom Brunel, the engineer of the Great Western Railway, who also designed the early steamships of the Victorian Age. On duty at a construction site, he stands against a background of enormous chain links, wearing a top hat, his jacket open to show a waistcoat, somewhat crumpled trousers, and a pair of stylish boots. There is a dandyish air about him, and his wry smile, helped by a long thin cigar, gives an aura of contentment with himself and the world. I bought the portrait some years ago, but if it is still on sale I imagine his cigar has been inked out by the anti-smoking and politically correct brigade.

Fanatical anti-smoking people seem to be taking over the civilised world. It's even worse in the United States, which has become a police state, run by the Anti-Nicotine Gestapo, of which much of the population are plain-clothes members. As with all such totalitarian regimes, the campaign was set going by middle-class liberals who for most of this century were trying to push Marxist-Leninist misery down the throats of everyone else. Having failed at that – though not for want of effort – they turned to anti-smoking and political correctness with a virulence that comes from scenting new blood.

The first Anti-Nicotine Police are seen on landing at JFK in New York. No-smoking signs are liberally plastered as you go through immigration and passport control, beyond which point tall men in black mackintoshes are on patrol. They wear peaked caps, and the logo of an armband which, instead of the swastika, has a red circle with a cigarette inside and a line running through it, meaning *verboten*. I saw a pair of them jump on a poor inoffensive-looking man, who put a false cigarette between his lips as an aid to *not* smoking, and they released him from the half nelson with great reluctance.

Another time I saw a Rottweiler tear a man's pocket away with such enthusiasm that it swallowed the cigarette before its keeper could take it away. Nobody laughed, except me, though I hurried along for fear of arrest.

At the hotel in Albany a room was set aside for smokers, as if they were lepers, though I doubt it's still tolerated. I was directed to it on booking in at the reception desk with a smouldering pipe in my mouth. The said room had a large Baconesque painting of a rotted lung on the wall, which I thought rather fine. In fact, the room was so peaceful I could write there undisturbed.

In Taos, New Mexico, I lit a cigar in a restaurant, a necessary consolation after a mediocre meal. A couple of anti-smokers at the next table asked me to put it out or move away. Since there was an ashtray before me I did neither, though I didn't relish the prospect of an unequal fight. They eventually went to another table, looking as if they had too much ordure in their heads to put up with the smell of a good cigar as well.

Send me your huddled masses, and they can go on huddling outside office buildings in the snow for a furtive guilt-inducing drag. I'm sure Emma Lazarus liked a puff or two.

Whatever happens in the Land of Liberty sooner or later comes to the country whose inhabitants never, never, never shall be slaves. The BBC has a ban on smoking in all its buildings, though I defy it whenever I'm to be interviewed. At their Nottingham studio I was requested not to smoke, and said in that case I wouldn't stay. It was free air time for them, after all. So they said I could smoke. Only Tony Benn had been allowed to do the same, and I was happy to be in the club of two.

Another disgraceful encroachment on the freedom of smokers is on Network South East, where no carriage is provided for those who want to take their fate into their own hands. I therefore go everywhere by car, and they can stuff their trains. You have to go over the Channel, to the comparative liberty of France, for such a facility. Or under the Channel, though that doesn't seem able to guarantee freedom from another sort of smoke. As for the London Underground, the only piece of technology that seems to work these days, is the recurring message of 'No Smoking' placed on every platform.

In the waiting hall of airports where no-smoking signs are well displayed I become a victim of passive coughing from non-smokers afflicted with ailments far more virulent than a whiff or two of my benign vegetarian tobacco. But I endure it, and don't give them black looks, or ask them to stop hawking and hacking. I would not, after all, like to see 'No Coughing' signs all over the place, or see them knocked about by the Anti-Coughing Police.

The erosion of freedom begins with small matters, and as those who legislate don't have any notion of enslavement, they are more determined to pursue the rest of us. If they are against smokers one day, they will be hounding others for more sinister reasons the next.

It could be, however, that anti-smoking rigours are ameliorating. One reads of the resurgence of cigar smoking in the United States, and a smoker must be encouraged and certainly amused by those photographs from France of people puffing unmolested in bars and restaurants under prominent 'No Smoking' signs. If I can fabricate a slogan to highlight the issue, let it be: 'Smokers of the world unite! You have nothing to lose but your ash!'

Sport and Nationalism

In February 1969, I received a letter from someone in Munich asking for my views on sport, with regard I suppose to the coming Olympic Games there. I can't recall his name, but it might have been my reply which resulted in an invitation to a conference in September 1972 called 'Against the Olympic Games'. People from all parts of Germany and a few other countries would be speaking in Cologne, among them the prize-winning novelist Heinrich Boll. My speech was an elaboration on what I said in the letter, and I was gratified that the large audiences saw something not quite right about the recently finished Games in Munich.

In days of old, sport was the king's pastime and pleasure, and now seems to be everybody's. By sport I mean the competitive sort, when men matched themselves against each other for so-called glory, or to gain cash, no matter how much superhuman effort was called upon, with its subsequent damage to the body.

There is, of course, genuine sport, enjoyable sport, non-competitive sport, as when I go cycling, or rowing on the river, or on an extended walk to test my endurance. This I find sporting enough, because if I am competing it is only with myself. When working in a factory in the old days a few of us youths would spend half our lunch hour kicking a tennis ball up and down the street, against each other, it's true, but for exercise and relaxation – I can hardly say fresh air!

Working men, who at one time met with their greyhounds or lurchers in a field to race them, did so with a kind of sporting instinct. Football clubs used to play what they called 'friendly' matches on Saturday afternoon. As children we would see who could get first to the top of a tree – a test of prowess and ingenuity, but nothing to bring out feelings of mass competitive sport.

Just as universal literacy was necessary to get people into the modern age, so competitive sport was a further cement to their enslavement. Every such distraction offered to the people was reached out for with alacrity, and one wonders why.

Even as late as the end of the nineteenth century a particularly vicious 'sport' was played in rural areas of south-east England, called 'kickshins', which is as good a description of it as any, because two men would stand face to face, arms on each other's shoulders, and take it in turns to give a kick at the opposite shins. The last to collapse would be the winner. Competitions were arranged between the champions of various villages, and local squires would bet on their favourites.

Sport has become big business. Allied to nationalism, it is also good propaganda. If England loses a football match against Germany the people are made to feel as if the Battle of Britain has just been refought, and the Union Jack in plain evidence symbolises a victory for the nation. The Battle of Waterloo was said to have been won on the playing fields of Eton, but in reality it was won by common soldiers guided by their officers, and finally clinched by the arrival of the Prussian General Blucher. One might just as well say that destiny settled the victory.

It often appears that sport has taken the place of war, if only as a way of keeping the national spirit alive during a time of so-called peace, thus preparing the national spirit for the eventuality of war.

The ceremony of the Olympic Games opens with the militaristic display of shields and flags, artillery salutes and fanfares. No sooner does the runner set out with his smoking torch than the honour of each nation is involved. At the risk of Clausewitz spinning in his grave, one might say that sport is diplomacy carried on by other means. It is encouraged in schools, and among adults who are either participants or spectators, in the hope perhaps of taking their minds from urgent social problems, or from the need to rebel when such problems are not solved quickly enough.

If England wins an international football match, or clears twenty gold-plated tin medals at some games or other, production goes up in the factories. Likewise, when the country lost at football, as in Mexico in 1970, Harold Wilson the prime minister was dispatched from power at the following election, losing to his Conservative opponent, Edward Heath, who must have been looking for victories from the current Olympic Games to increase his chances at the next election.

You might think that England's sporting prowess is linked to the floating pound. One lost goal and a few cents are chipped off sterling in the financial arenas. A few centimetres off the high jump, and a left-wing demonstration gets too close to the American Embassy in Grosvenor Square.

The defeat of England means long faces for a week, if radio and television have their way, the media pandering to the lowest common denominator of nationalism when it comes to sport. Exulting in what is called victory, they hide as best they can so-called defeat, or turn surly and nasty against the losers.

True sport, and there is such a thing, is not to set people competing against each other in deed and thought, but to work together as a team, in the conquest of some arduous enterprise or obstacle. To climb a mountain 'because it's there' is under-standable, but not to race others to the summit. A dozen people making their way across South America to gather scientific information can be good, but not if two such groups set out to discover who can do it quickest, or get to know most. That is immoral and stupid. Only has only to recollect Captain Scott's race to the South Pole against Amundsen, and the disaster it led to.

If an athlete jumps 16 feet, and gets a piece of gold with his name stamped on it – in smaller letters than the name of his country – he will become a national hero for a few weeks, which is something ludicrous, if not pathetic. Surrounded by flags and spectators, the performance of his act turns into a national ritual, with everyone getting some semi-sexual power-drive out of the fact that his jump would be their jump if only they had trained for it, and hadn't recently eaten such big amounts of junk food.

They feel his power to be their own, see him – or her – for a moment, as themselves, as if at that instant a government minister came into the stands and ordered them to get up and then jump 16 feet, the same as their idolised athlete, they would no doubt try to do so. If some mechanism could be fitted into every television set and, immediately after the big jump, a voice called to all viewers: 'Now YOU jump – for the good of your country, because those in all other countries are doing the same, and the honour of your nation is at stake' – the nation would jump as one person. The nation in armchairs would become the nation in arms.

The Olympic Games cannot be considered as anything other than a mass rally. Under the guise of international friendly competition the same old nationalist values and rivalries are encouraged. It has nothing to do with real friendship between countries, or between the people of these countries.

As soon as a man participates, either at the actual place or vicariously through the medium of television, radio or the newspapers, he loses his individuality and, with unreasonable yearnings in his heart, becomes part of his nation.

Sport in a totalitarian state drills the individual into subservience to the totalitarian system. In a so-called democratic state competitive sport is used in the same way. The participants appear to be competing primarily for themselves and not their country, but as soon as they enter the stadium or arena they are as much representatives of their country as those who belong to a totalitarian system. The media sees to that, and so do the people who so readily take up its message.

The Olympic torch is a symbol of the oppression of the free human spirit. All sensible people should flee from the burning flame carried along the highway. When it reaches the stadium, and the crowd roars with fierce delight, the only human response is to get beyond sight and earshot.

Gladiatorial combats in Ancient Rome, chariot races in Constantinople, bull fights in modern Spain, and the Olympic Games in whatever place they are held, signify that any benevolence in the spirit of man is under threat, the body wrecked and abused, the heart broken.

War is the result of giving in to the atavistic delight of getting your hands at someone else's throat. It is a weakness of intellect and sensibility. Mass competitive sport, in encouraging the survival of the fittest (though often the most stupid) turns the arena into a jungle, where the fittest are used to calculate the human measurement of both personal and nationalistic aspirations.

The truly civilised ought instinctively to abominate it, and with reason protest against it, but no sane voice can be heard above the frantic decibels of noise from the crowd. Civilisation is jeopardised by contests of the arena, the Olympic torch lighting up the hollow eyes of the dictator, and turning all faces ecstatically towards the national flag.

After the murder of the eleven Israeli athletes by Palestinian terrorists, the voices of commentators from the Olympic Games in Munich took on tones of real obscenity, an obscenity of the spirit that from now on should be recalled as representative of all Olympic Games. The resumption of those Games in such haste by a host country unwilling to give up its pride and its financial investments, and by athletes exploiting their physical prowess at the expense of all human feeling, emphasised their true purpose. The continuation of the Games was also the most effective way of drawing a curtain on the atrocity, a victory for terrorism.

During the conference many people spoke against the Games in a general sort of way, but I was astounded at not hearing anyone refer to the murder of the Israelis, as if they thought that to do so would be taking an unfair advantage of our hosts. As the final speaker, however, I made a special point of the event, which ought to have been previously condemned by everyone.

Why they were so shy of doing so, I'll never know. Maybe they feared that an interminable discussion would have ensued to stall the proceedings. On the other hand, perhaps many of the speakers decided individually to pull back from the issue, on the assumption that some in the audience felt sympathetic to the murderers. If I went in where angels fear to tread, it was not because nobody had gone before me, but to wonder why they hadn't stated from the beginning the reason for all of us being there.

In Bohemia

We were driven out of medieval Prague on a thundery afternoon by a Czech writer in his Skoda car, through the lush and undulating countryside of Bohemia, to the Château of Dobris, a writers' rest and convalescent home. Myself, Ruth Fainlight and our infant son David had been invited to stay a week, perhaps in recompense for a couple of my books whose royalties could not be paid into an English bank.

Our accommodation needed two glances to take in its extent. It was the size of a hall, and not very good oil paintings of various ancestors on the walls made it seem like a room in a museum. At the furthest point from our bed was David's large high-sided crib, a piece of furniture in which many an effete and princely darling of the archduchess might have gone to sleep. He took to his territory with the proprietorship of an eighteen-month-old, but the first morning he woke with joy at sunlight flooding through windows that, I suppose, were too big for curtains, and rattled the railing of his domain with such enthusiasm that it collapsed, and he fell onto a floor – an infinite distance below – that was no less hard for being tiled in an attractive geometrical pattern. Indignant shrieks woke us earlier than hoped for, and although a length of string soon made the railing safe, his exuberance on subsequent mornings was understandably restrained.

Mythological characters in the French garden flanked one of the walks. A middle-aged irascible cherub carried a load of fruit on his back (or maybe coal), another wore a hunting hat, and one was humped over a cudgel, or crutch, vice inscribed over all three faces. Others were taking part in the Rape of Ariadne, and in the death of this or that Parnassian creature. Hercules carried a cosh, Perseus a chiv, while Sisyphus managed his burden of a boulder as if to prove that the world of legend wasn't altogether shy of hard labour. Lascivious nymphs and satyrs seemed to be rubbing themselves off against a tree stump. A jaguar mounted (or rended) a cow. A lion rended (or mounted) a horse, while the fountains played water music among flowerbeds, lawns, embankments and sylvan pools. So many busy monstrosities, heading for a bad end, illustrated the fragility of civilised existence.

A flight of steps led to a vast terrace recalling the film *Last Year in Marienbad*, such emptiness driving me beyond the French park to an English wood. The former owners of the estate, having friends and relations in every opulent nook and prosperous enclave of Europe, had for hundreds of years exchanged presents of hunting dogs, fighting cocks, trees and plants and – no doubt – women. With a few score trees from England aesthetically surplus to requirements the archduke had his peasants lay out an English wood.

The atmosphere was not entirely English. From a height among the trees in early evening a two-pronged lake with steep shores was visible, flat and mirror-like, black shapes of small islands so clearly reflected that afterwards it was hard to know whether or not the photograph was upside down. Gothic, silent and eerie, fireflies sprang up as at the touch of typewriter keys. A ring around the moon in the shining lake created an erotic atmosphere that few strolling couples could have resisted, maybe ending in a Mayerling-style suicide pact.

Behind the main house kids paddled naked in a large rectangular pool, their mothers watching over them as they lay in their bikinis to get a tan. The Princes Colloredo-Mansfeld could never have imagined that lawyers, writers, scientists or, worst of all, housewives, would put the pool to such use.

David went naked into the water, but the other children were no more friendly to him than their parents were towards us.

Maybe it was the language problem, our knowledge of Czech being nil. So we watched solitary David in his foot or so of water, which clearly showed his pink legs and bottom, wondering what he should do next.

The look of concentration on his features, of something about to be achieved, was not unfamiliar, but why he had waited till it was too late to do anything about it, and at that moment defecated into their pristine paddling pool, I'll never know. Maybe in his babyish yet tidy mind he decided that those looking at him so disapprovingly were responsible for his falling out of the crib that morning, and that this was a perfect act of revenge. As a foreigner the women eyed him surreptitiously, so they could not fail to notice the shoal of brown objects that dribbled from between his legs.

Seeing their pool polluted by this malicious little capitalist brat acting with the same flamboyant disregard as those concrete statues, or with the aristocratic panache of the former owner's children, the women gathered their little offspring up with, I thought, unjustified disdain, while Ruth and I fished for the offending detritus and dumped it between the rose bushes. Should the pool need to be drained then the writers could pay for it from the two per cent of their royalties that went to the château's upkeep. Publishers also contributed to the fund, which made us feel even better.

In 1942 the last of the Colloredo-Mansfelds was ordered to Germany by the Nazis, where he pined for his beloved château, and died soon afterwards from an unspecified illness. His family hoped to return some day, but when the Red Army came they scattered to America and West Germany, a few going to England. The Czech writer who had driven us from Prague said that the last of the line had collaborated with the Germans.

Frick, the syphilitic and demented Nazi, made the place his headquarters during the war, as Reichsprotector of Bohemia, and signed thirty thousand death warrants. When peace came he was put on trial in Prague, and then hanged, screaming his innocence.

Frick's SS guards had their canteen in the gloomy cellar where we took our meals. A small Union Jack for me, and a Stars and Stripes for Ruth, were put on our table, and each time we hid them by a radiator, not caring to be distinguished by our nationalities, but at every meal they were back in place, perhaps as signs that we were to be avoided by the other guests.

The chairs we sat on in the library would, in an English country house, have had pieces of fading red rope across their arms, and the tables we wrote at would have been beyond a cordon with a label hanging from them. A Japanese vase mounted on four dragons, a Buddha, a Ming vase, and a dozen eighteenth-century prints on golden silk wallpaper adorned the place. The great writers of Czechoslovakia – Kafka, Jaroslav Hasek and the Brothers Capek – had died before they could step into such an inheritance, though I don't suppose they would have wanted much to do with it, in any case.

Many books in the archduke's library were on hunting, war, history and travel. There were several hundred volumes of Alexandre Dumas, with sets of Dickens and Sir Walter Scott, as well as the works of Oscar Wilde, a couple of H G Wells, a stray Jack London and some Rousseau, all leather-bound and with the ex-libris: 'principis de Colloredo-Mansfeld' under a coat of arms of shield and two lions, with a crown above. An antiquarian book merchant of London or Amsterdam would have watered at the mouth, but they were safe here, and if even to think of stealing one or two proves I was tempted, I did not want to end up in a salt mine.

While sitting to write our picture postcards David played safely within the raised sides of the large billiard table, where he enjoyed crawling to the edge and launching the archduke's balls across the floor.

At midday in the gardens water as ever splashed in the sultry air, and attenuating cracks of thunder drowned the noise of bees. People were in their quarters or eating in the restaurant, and, walking along the corridor on my way to call for Ruth and David, I passed the room of an eighty-year-old Czech writer, the only person who had so far been friendly to us. The open door showed him about to begin typing, though he only looked at the machine, as if wondering whether his next chapter would get by the censors.

In the evening thousands of watts burned from chandeliers in the great hall but, needing only a section of it, we were unable to find any light that would work singly, and so economise with the current. But on Saturday night the gilded youth of the Writers' Union, with no such thoughts, rolled the archduke's enormous carpet back, and set the radiogram going. They also brought tape recorders, and the beat of jazz began, ragtime New Orleans, swing, boogie-woogie, and on to the frontiers of Cool. Little girls and mature women asked young men onto the floor, or danced with each other.

Bottles of wine, beer and Cuban rum spread over the tables, any contribution gladly accepted. We had gone into Prague the previous day and bought two bottles of Scotch with our convertible currency, so when that too went into the kitty we were acknowledged for the first time, though with smiles more than words, as the yes-men writers and their families went on with their feverish weekend hop.

I wondered which of England's stately homes might be chosen for writers to carouse in. Woburn? Hatfield House? Montecute? Wollaton Hall for the Nottingham Writers' Club? The trades unions would get there first, though it was never too early to put in a claim, or to dream of such a possibility from the middle of Bohemia. However, I would rather not have such a facility if it meant being told what to write, which it surely would.

Walking to the village to buy stamps, with David in his pushchair, local people passing on the road looked as if they would like to hang me from the nearest tree. As far as they knew I was one of the writers who boozed and lounged all day in the sun, and wore out the furniture in the mansion of their former masters, whom they now remembered as having been generous and paternalistically caring. Such as myself were living off their backs, and giving comfort to the regime that oppressed them.

There was enough of me in them, and of them in me, for me to know what dark and vengeful thoughts ran in their minds. One day the men of the village, and the women too, would march up to the château with their scythes and pitchforks, and slaughter whatever bone-idle bastards they could lay their hands on. Or, if they were merciful – which was belied by such expressions – they'd send them back to their one-room flats in the city where they belonged.

As long as they don't rise up in the next couple of days, I thought, by which time I would be gone.

On the Bike in France

'Have you written any good books lately?' the friendly passport official asked when I leaned my ten-speed Carlton Raleigh – red, Grand Prix, made in Worksop, England, green panniers at rear – against his box. Straining at the first two-hundred-metre hill beyond the Channel I was to wonder whether the title mentioned might not be the last, having cycled little since the age of eighteen, a very long time ago.

My usual exit from the island is by car. In fact, I always make sure there is enough petrol in the tank to get me well into France at a minute's notice, no matter what the government of the moment. It's like a prisoner able to have the cell door slightly open, or a rope under his bed, or a file in the deepest part of his pillow.

The bike was roped to a steam pipe in the belly of the ship, with a prayer that the Range Rover a few feet away wouldn't break loose and slide against it in a rough sea. The decks and all interiors were crowded with day trippers, but for much of the crossing I shouldered my way around the duty free, looking for tobacco, which, being Players' Medium Flake, meant staring at Nottingham Castle on the lid whenever a fill was needed.

Cyclists were let off first, the French passport and customs officers waving me by as if coast or frontier didn't exist. I paralleled the main road beyond Boulogne, through a mostly built-up route to Samer, where I stopped for coffee served in a cup and saucer and not, as on the boat, in a plastic container of acorn water.

A bike would clock up a lot more mileage in a day than the fifteen or twenty on foot, guaranteeing a change of landscape or locality before night. Also, pedalling was exercise, whereas walking could be drudgery. My plan was to travel in as straight a line as possible by lanes and tracks, thus avoiding traffic on arterial roads, to the old battlefields of the Somme between Albert and Bapaume.

Lanes went more often over hills, little worry on looking at maps before setting out, but faced with the first steep incline after Samer, I got off to push. Not having handled a modern bike meant trouble switching the ten gears from one to another and, stopping to select the right one for tackling the hill, the chain came off. Recalling the carefree days of the simple three-speed, my hands were soon blackened with oil trying to fix it.

Two cyclists stopped to ask what the trouble was: lean athletic middle-aged men, professionally kitted out in coloured caps and smart capes, their sporting velocipedes having two waterbottles on each frame instead of one.

Seeing my difficulty, one of them unbuttoned a pannier, took out rubber gloves so as not to soil his fine hands, and got the chain back into its appropriate sprocket in seconds. He also showed ways of controlling the gears, and in our chat said they were surgeons from a London teaching hospital on a spin to Burgundy.

They were soon so far ahead as not to see me in their rear mirrors walking the rest of the hill, intending to practise my new expertise on the descent. One thing I knew, that if mangled at some future time in an accident, I could have no better surgeons to fit me back into one piece.

The altitude of a bicycle, higher than that of a windscreen, showed more of the scenery, though everything has its price, for a steady rain began. Welcome after a summer drought, or in the desert, it was not so for me, my cape of such impermeable material that sweat rolled from within the sleeves and onto my hands as copiously as water from heaven flowed down the outside. The saturation to my face was uncomfortable because of a beard – later to be scraped away on deciding I was too old to wear one.

I'd hoped to make the first day short by putting up at Hucqueliers, twenty miles inland, but learned in the café that there was no accommodation, so I slogged on over the green uplands of Artois. Ceilings of grey cloud continue the downpour, and I stopped to eat Kentish apples plucked from a tree at home, blessing Eve for ever more as the sweet taste went down. The occasional car left plenty of room on overtaking, far safer – in the days before helmets – than on the twisting lanes in England.

The first day or so on such a jaunt made me wonder what I was doing, and why I was where I was. Preparation was the best part of the trip, so why hadn't I left it at that, and stayed with the familiar books and objects in my comfortable room, instead of grumbling across soaking landscape like a drowning rat? For miles I saw no other person, there being fewer houses between French villages than in England, where cottages are everywhere.

My cantankerous sense of isolation was fought off by the spending of energy, which brought back the elation of being alone. The freedom of an empty mind, of its utter thought-lessness, was the perfect existence, my only aim to find a room in which to dry off, stretch out, and eat.

If there had been nothing at the Hotel Moderne in Fruges I would have begged a barn at the nearest farm and slept in conditions luxurious to the men of the Great War, but the response was that they did have a room, and before first looking at it, as might be the case when arriving by car, I drank a bottle of Stella at the bar, any shelter being more than good enough, and talked to the youngish, saturnine manager, who asked how I had come to know of his hotel. I'd got the mention out of a *Guide Bleu*, but didn't say the date was 1920. He told me to shelter my bike under an awning in the courtyard, adding: 'The dogs are harmless.'

A pair of ferocious-looking brutes shared a kennel to the left of the archway, and at my appearance Number One, all chops foaming, ran the radius of action almost to the opposite side of the entrance, and half-throttled itself at the end of a none-too-strong-looking chain. I had no sympathy when its whine of disappointment ended in a pathetic choking sound.

'Get back, you bastard!' To my surprise he did but, before reaching the villa-style kennel, Number Two was already leaping across the space, should I try a runner in the interim. Stern instructions sent him back to the kennel as well, but Number One was on its way out again, flat pads going like a supercharged steam engine.

Wanting them to let me go by, I tried flattery, I tried bullying, I tried diplomacy in French and English, and threatened them with God's wrath in Spanish, but neither would cease their insane determination to use my tobacco-kippered ankles for their evening hors-d'oeuvres. The proprietor was either laughing quietly at my problem, or throwing his hands up at such timidity, for the racket was unmistakable.

If I tried a leap through the arch – though how, with a laden bike? – one or both would make a meal of me before I could sample the delicious food already simmering inside the hostelry. As their Box and Cox antics continued, one out and the other back, then the other out and back (being passed half-way), it seemed that the only possibility of reaching the courtyard in safety would be to push the bike through the lounge and dining room of the hotel, but such a course seemed too cowardly, and all I could do was stand there, hoping that neither chain would come apart as they snarled back and forth.

I recalled a sentence from *The Last Days of Pompeii* by Bulwer-Lytton: 'He endured the bitterest curse of noble natures – humiliation' till inspiration decided how I would put a stop to it. Without thought, but under a sudden downrush of rain, I shouted the few words of German heard in films about the Second World War: '*Raus! Schnell! Raus! Arbeit macht frei!*'

Hard to know whether they understood, probably not, but the hesitation at my change of tone was long enough for me to slip in clear of their fangs.

Lock the wheel, off with the panniers, and to the bar for another drink. A cramp in my right thigh was the only effect of the forty miles. The pain was intense, but the swearing worse, which soon got rid of it. An ample dinner, after a bath and change of shirt, was croquis St Jacques, then pork steaks (salt on everything) and crème caramel for dessert, smoothed down with a bottle of house red. Because the exchange rate was at an all-time high, the meal, room and breakfast came to just over £10.

The cheaper the hotel the bigger the pot of coffee for breakfast and so, well satisfied, I went to retrieve my bike from between the jaws of the early rising Cerberii. The distinction of being the only writer to be killed by dogs, while it had been high on the achievement list last night, was now less so because of their previous failures, though the noise must have stirred the whole town.

Refuelled with good food and a long sleep, I walked towards them with my bicycle, turned as if to go back, then charged through, the bike frame covering my right flank. I was on the road before they could get at me, though Number One came close, their howls of execration following me almost as far as Agincourt.

Sleepy *Azincourt*, a few miles down the road, gave off no sound, cattle munching on the one-time battlefield. After mulling on those flights of arrows from 1415, I mounted my Raleigh steed and resumed a southwesterly course, using the excellent maps of the *Institut Geographique National* at the 1:100,000 scale, which showed sufficient contours for a cyclist to make out the landscape. Signposting was good enough, but a stop at forks and crossroads to be sure of taking the right lane or track, and to look around, added interest as well as breath to the monotony of pedalling.

I pushed uphill, another watershed mounted, hoping the brake cables wouldn't snap during the steep coast down. Little more than a tractor or a farmer's car went by, always a friendly wave as the driver took care to avoid me on his way to tend the endless fertility of the soil. Woods on the horizon formed a backdrop for sleek cattle or huge cylindrical bales of hay, every few miles a village with church, café, bakery and general shop selling food for a picnic.

The sun's warmth lunched on grey clouds, sky clearer as the coast was left behind. Propelling myself agreeably along, not knowing where the next bed would be, nor much caring, made me wonder why I hadn't done such a trip before: my twenty-year-old son had taken a Kawasaki, and given his pushbike to me.

At the Café de la Poste in the little town of Pas-en-Artois, a room of bed, wardrobe and sink was welcome after a day's perspiring ride. My top-floor window looked at tiles about to dribble off the next roof, a vine trellis creeping up the wall. At the back I was away from traffic, and undisturbed by pop music and space invader machines in the late-night bar.

A long push uphill next morning led towards the one-time Western Front, a dead straight road after Souastre, crows disagreeing loudly in the trees. Tarmac hotted up as the sky cleared to give good visibility across open fields.

In the café-hotel at Foncquevillers (Fonky Villas, to the Sherwood Foresters) coffee was brought by a woman wearing curlers and carpet slippers, maybe the granddaughter of a soldier who had gone over the top to be seen no more. I wanted milk in my coffee, so she came from behind the bar with a tin of Libby's, two holes punched in as if by a knitting needle, and filled my cup to the brim. The hotel was empty, but would be crowded with ex-soldiers on the night before 1 July, who came to celebrate their survival of the Great Offensive, and to renew old friendships.

The fields were planted with corn, potatoes and barley, no reminders of the long-gone battle as I ate lunch, but an aura of desolation and sadness hovered nevertheless. My 1:10,000 trench map, carefully preserved in a plastic case, covered the area of the failed attack, the German defences only three or four hundred yards beyond the line. The British soldiers had been in their trenches for a week, miserably wet, overworked and bombarded and badly fed. At half-past seven in the morning they went over the top with 60lb of kit on their backs, and rifles they hardly had time to fire, each man in fear yet also with élan at getting onto open ground at last.

A few minutes later most were dead or wounded, for they went at a slow pace (how else?), barked-at to stay in line, and found the German barbed wire hardly cut after a week of shelling. Twelve hundred were shot down by German machine gunners and their artillery, while another battalion of Sherwood Foresters was destroyed on the southern flank of the Gommecourt salient, a black day for Nottingham, as well as other places, because twenty-two thousand were killed on the twenty-mile front of attack, and thirty-five thousand were wounded. A few soldiers got through the wire and into enemy trenches, only to be driven out or taken prisoner by nightfall. Most lay dead and dying between the lines.

The heart-breaking monotony of so many crosses in the impeccably looked-after cemeteries was varied by an occasional Star of David. Every mile or so I leaned my bike against the concrete balustrade and walked among their collective acreages, which seemed to contain more British dead than parts of the country they came from. At the entrance to each necropolis was a remembrance book in which visitors could write their comments, but at one place it had been cut from its chain and stolen. Why? By whom?

Touring such places on a bicycle seemed right, a forty-mile circuit through Gommecourt and Pusieux, down to the valley of the Ancre and up to Courcelette and Martinpuich. High Wood was fought over for weeks, its trees reduced to stumps and splinters, now densely regrown and well fenced. A sign protected private rights, and kept people out of danger from unexploded shells and mortar bombs, which still maim souvenir hunters and the unwary. Captain Robert Graves of the Royal Welch Fusiliers was wounded by a burst of shrapnel in July 1916, and reported killed in action on his 21st birthday, but was alive in Majorca seventy years later.

On to Flers (the first appearance of British tanks) and Longueval, to Montauban, Mametz and Fricourt, then into Albert for the night, after a dry and brilliant day. At the Hotel de la Paix supper began with a tomato salad, and when I asked for more garlic the chef in his white hat came into the dining room, stood disdainfully over my table, chopped up two cloves, and sprinkled it on. A television above the crockery dresser played an endless quick-moving *policier* drama, which did not stop me from lingering over the usual coffee and duty-free cigar, and looking at the map for the next day's move.

Two mosquitoes, who'd had the bedroom to themselves all day, and were now famished from their amorous manoeuvres, divebombed my skin, but after a characteristic cutting-off of engines to make a landing, seemed reluctant to bite at well-garlicked flesh, which would have sent them away coughing fit to die.

I pulled the sheet over my head to shut out the noise, but at dawn a loud singing indicated that they had in fact stayed in, for which cunning move they paid more than I did. A quick struggle turned them into blobs on the sheet of the previous occupant's blood, and allowed me two more hours of sleep.

From Albert, south through Morlancourt, I crossed the dilatory Somme at Sailly, an elderly fisherman painted against bushes upstream. Dove noises came from the woods, then silence except for the wind whispering the information that it can sometimes howl. Farm tracks and quiet minor roads – cattle with numbers clamped on their ears – took me to the Australian memorial and cemetery near Villers Brettonneux, a high spot marking the launch of the offensive on 8 August 1918. On that 'black day of the German Army' a breakthrough was made, due to the genius of the Australian commander Sir John Monash who, an architect in civil life, weighed every detail with intelligence and imagination, and used tanks and aircraft in combination for the first time.

Nervous of traffic on cycling into the Amiens conurbation, I needn't have been, and soon found the house of the poet Jacques Darras, who put me up for a couple of nights. Struggling against sleep, after a long and convivial supper, I wrote the first draft of a poem called 'Stones in Picardy' into my notebook.

On Sunday morning I cycled around *Les Hortillonages*, market gardens on the outskirts intersected by channels from the Somme. Farmers, manoeuvring their skiffs, sold fresh and colourful produce to people crowding the banks.

The serpentine course to Dieppe – arduous but rewarding – went along lanes so quiet they seemed laid out for my private use. Some remote villages couldn't have altered much since described in stories by Guy de Maupassant. Not finding a hotel in Oisement, I rode 7 kilometres along the main road through a sudden and inexplicable mist, scared that a lorry coming up behind would miss my feeble light.

At Le Transloy was a place listed in Michelin, so there I stopped, and got my bike under cover by pushing it through the front rooms of the old coaching inn, to leave it in the kitchen at the back. Cooking had already begun for supper, a Norman speciality of fish laced with pepper. After a long day I slept like a stone encased in fur, dreams too thick to be remembered.

A two-hundred-metre ridge barred the way to Dieppe, covered by a forest called Eu, not necessary to pronounce in asking directions, since I found my way to the top by reading the map. When a largish fly settled on it in the sun I could see the contours clearly through its transparent lace wings.

No vehicles passed, either coming or going, the cool lane so subtly engineered that for once it was unnecessary to dismount and push, though in any case I was much fitter than at the beginning. A muscular bullock in an orchard at the summit stood on hind legs quietly stripping an apple tree, while I was on the verge eating my bread, ham and chocolate croissant, and gurgling a litre of water. France is ideal for picnics, the best of food for sale in nearly every village, which makes eating a pleasure as soon as the hunger clock strikes.

After stolidly finishing all fruit within reach of its snout the bullock looked at me, who could eat no more, then began its depredations on the next tree, again managing the feat of standing tall on two back legs.

I could have biked on for weeks, but a timetable in a café near Dieppe told me that a boat for Newhaven would leave at five o'clock. On the last miles along the main road even juggernauts gave me the space of a car when overtaking, so that I didn't need to bring up my favourite adage that you're always too young to die. As usual after hurrying there was time to spare. A gaggle of club cyclists, having their last drinks at a café on the quayside, gave a companionable wave.

Cars queued but cyclists were allowed on first. After 350 kilometres I felt fit, whereas the same number of days in the car would have left me bilious and dyspeptic. Food and lodging had been the one expense, and locomotion was free. I took more money than was needed for the cost of £150 from door to door.

Crossing on the *Senlac* in the middle of September, there were many carefree passengers (no trippers this time) and it seemed – a glassy blue surface warmed by the sun – that we were moving between two islands in the tropics, a rare manifestation in the Channel.

St Pagoire and the Anniversary
of the Revolution

In the village of St Pagoire, where I live for as much of the year
as can be managed, a statue of the French Republic stands in
the small central square. Holding the torch of liberty high, she is
surrounded by a concrete parapet, and three circles of specially
grown flowers in red, white and blue for the two-hundredth
anniversary of the Revolution. Behind, blocking off any possible
retreat, is the fortress-like structure of the thirteenth-century
church, hemmed in by buttresses and narrow streets. In front
stands the town hall, so it is no accident that she turns her back
on religion, and faces the edifice of social and national
responsibility. As consolation the church is given a star of
commendation in the regional *Guide Bleu*, whereas the typical and
unpretentious *mairie* gets no mention.

Half in love with her, I dream of climbing over the parapet and
onto the pedestal so as to get closer to the charms of her delectable
poitrine, which is more pleasant to look on than the multiplicity of
living mammaries sunbathing on the nearest beach.

If I made the attempt, on some dark night, merry on wine
from the surrounding vineyards, no doubt the local people would
not like it, and in any case I would be sure to break a leg in the
subsequent fall. So I glance at her in silence on my way through
the *place*, and wonder about her thoughts on the coming two-
hundredth anniversary of what must have been the most
momentous event in the village's history. She wasn't, of course,

present at the time of the Revolution, having been unveiled – I think that's the word – in 1904, to honour the Republic rather than the Revolution.

An equally potent symbol for the people of St Pagoire could be the snail, and that for a very good reason. In the early part of the twentieth century, the viticulturists of the Languedoc were ruined by the phylloxera, and there were demonstrations and riots in nearby Beziers. People were killed when Clemenceau brought in the army, but the soldiers of the Seventeenth Régiment, many of whom came from the same region, mutinied, and set up the cry: '*On assassine nos frères!*' – 'We are killing our brothers!' – for which sentiments they were to serve in a remote part of Algeria as punishment. By then the people of St Pagoire were so hungry there was little left to eat except the humble escargot, and local T-shirts have ever since displayed this incongruous logo.

Whether the statue of the Republic broods on such events is hard to say. She was too young at the time to notice – a mere toddler – but if she thinks anything these days it might be to wonder at the lotto games that go on three nights a week for much of the year in the principal café, a couple of dark alleys away. People motor in from miles around, so that two nearby halls have been opened by the same proprietor.

Thus, without realising, in our search for an inconspicuous place with no outstanding fame or notoriety (nor any other English inhabitants) we landed in the Las Vegas of the Languedoc. Walking along the deserted main street at night you see figures behind the windows intently 'looking down' on their cards, and placing grains of corn as numbers are called. Everyone is still and silent, as if in a glass case of some provincial museum illustrating life in another age by using doll-like figures. Last Christmas Eve every lotto seat was taken, while outside one or two old ladies made their way slowly to midnight mass in a church big enough to seat twenty villages these days.

For a revolution to be consolidated into the same sort of social order that existed before (name the system what you will) it must be celebrated every year, in case anyone should get the idea that another might be needed. In the meantime, hope can be sustained by a fling in the Halls of Lotto, and the possibility of driving home afterwards with half a pig or a few thousand francs prize – or a hole in the pocket. Since they can already afford to eat cake, let them now play lotto.

St Pagoire, like many villages in this part of France, had a large Protestant community at the time of the Revolution, two hundred out of twelve hundred. Of the Protestant families today people say: 'They own all the businesses, and only marry among themselves', something I seem to have heard before. Their temple is closed and neglected, but in 1789 the Protestants had better reason than most to welcome the Storming of the Bastille. The village lived from the soil, growing wheat and vegetables, olives, almonds and also, of course, grapes. Today the vine dominates, a monoculture that the government, with little success, would like people to discontinue and take to growing asparagus.

Prior to the Revolution the Languedoc was a prosperous area of France, mainly from the manufacture of silks and woollens. 'Denim' cloth got its name through being made in Nîmes. New markets were opening up in the Levant and – through Spain – in Mexico and Peru. Thousands of workmen were employed in Nîmes, Montpellier and many smaller towns. A developing bourgeoisie, predominantly Protestant, was influenced by the ideas of the Encyclopaedists. Over two hundred people subscribed to the quarto edition of Diderot's encyclopaedia in Nîmes alone.

The Suffolk farmer Arthur Young travelled in France on the eve of the Revolution, and wrote a book that became required reading in French schools through much of the nineteenth century, he being regarded as a reliable and impartial witness to conditions before the Great Event. He noted the prosperity of the Languedoc as opposed to the destitution in other places, and of the area in which St Pagoire stands. 'A very fine country, a vale of six or eight leagues' extent, all cultivated; a beautiful mixture of vines, mulberries, olives, towns, and scattered houses, the whole bounded by gentle hills and cultivated to their tops.'

By 1789 the age of plenty was over, however, because in 1786 England took over the trade in the Levant, and Spain closed its frontier to French goods two years later. Mass unemployment ensued, and a law of 1787 confirmed the exclusion of Protestants from the liberal professions in France, and therefore from all political life.

The Revolution at St Pagoire was mainly a process of administrative reform, though one man was killed in a brawl before the religious factions settled down. In an anti-clerical gesture all villages in the region named after saints were relabelled, St Pagoire becoming Pargoire l'Herault.

In talking about the two-hundredth anniversary celebrations, the man who runs the hardware store, where everything from big butane gas 'bombs' to Tippex and blotting paper was sold, shrugged and said: 'It happened a long time ago, didn't it?' There was irony in his tone but he meant that people live too much in the present to worry about what went on in past times.

You need never leave the village for the necessaries of life, because there are two shops for everything, so many that one wonders how they make a living. There's a doubling up of butcher, baker, grocer, hairdresser, doctor, and masseur. So many in a place of twelve hundred people gives the atmosphere of a small town rather than a village. Until recently there was a railway station, but in 1970 the French equivalent of Beeching plied his axe. Every family in the village seems to have a few hectares of vineyard, which means that at the time of the harvest, or *vendange*, tractors pulling huge vats of grapes rattle continuously under our windows during the hours of daylight, which sounds reminiscent – or so I say in my more anti-social moments – of tumbrils travelling along the Paris streets during the Terror.

Noise and prosperity go together, and why not? The young on their two-stroke Mobylettes take delight in rodeoing around the village – girls often, with another riding pillion. In early evening, standing on a hill after a peaceful walk through the vineyards, it sounds as if all the hornets in the world are having their annual meeting in the streets below.

Once or twice a day the 'Allo, allo' voice of the town crier echoes from megaphones on prominent corners, calling the village's attention to a *boules* match at half-past six, or telling that a van of shellfish is waiting for customers in the square.

So much for wanting to live in a quiet French village, yet we knew that being surrounded by other houses would make it safer to leave for months at a time. Our French friends have a small isolated house two miles away, which they are slowly making habitable, and they once went there to find that thieves had taken the new doors and roof tiles, as well as the shutters from their hinges.

It's always good to have friendly neighbours to keep an eye on the place. We made more friends in a month than after eighteen years in an English village, where I was more than once warned by a farmer to get off land he considered to be totally his. At least in France the Revolution put paid to that. In the first few weeks at St Pagoire we were welcomed by these neighbours with a box of choice grapes, and on 8 May they invited us across the road to celebrate victory in Europe with a couple of bottles from their own vineyard.

A few miles away the *garrigue* begins, a stony undulating heath crossed by barely motorable tracks. A double puncture from the flinty shards, or getting stuck in a chocolate-coloured patch after rain, and you would need to find your way out on foot, but it is a botanist's delight, for you are surrounded by clover, morning glory, honeysuckle, cornflowers, and poppies between stones and bushes, and angels' hair grasses flowing in a wind that lets no trees grow.

We are paving part of our garden, so drive to a place of flat slate-like stones, of such an extent that you might think a city once stood there. At our rate of collecting the job will take years, but it keeps the muscles taut with the lifting, and provides a motive for visits to the empty and mysterious area, vandalising though the task may be. In a similar terrain north-west of Montpellier you find deep untended tombs of the Visigoths, who once inhabited the region.

I sometimes sit there and write, the air scented with rosemary and thyme, and once the car engine has been switched off, and the noise of a couple of military jets on their daily low-flying exercise has died away, there is a silence that will hardly be the theme of the Revolutionary celebrations in the village, according to the programme of events posted on the wall of the town hall, whose windows overlook my favourite statue.

Activities have already started, and the cafés and shops are decorated with tricoloured bunting and streamers. Sweets on a market stall – *Bons-bons Revolutionaires* – are displayed in three bands of red, white and blue, as if tempting my topless statue to step down and try one.

Driving through a back lane of the village a few days ago we were confronted by an unexpected procession of children. Marshalled by their teachers, they flowed past in their red-white-and-blue dresses, and sporting Liberty Caps, some girls powdered and mobcapped in the dress of the time – fifty angelic faces heartily singing the *Marseillaise*, one tiny black boy with glasses voicing the words ecstatically.

After songs and dances by the local folklore group on the morning of 14 July, in the costume of the Revolutionary Era, a Tree of Liberty will be planted. As a long-term Republican I shall certainly attend, and in any case there are free drinks and *coquillages* afterwards. At the continuous '*animations*' of the 13th and 14th there will be more dances, and further samplings of wines from the region, going on to a grand evening of – what else? – lotto.

Childrens' games and competitions will be held on the Boulevard de la Victoire – a rather grand name for a street (albeit wide) on the edge of the village. Another inauguration of the Tree of Liberty is followed by a game of *pétanque*, a bonfire and open-air dancing of, I suspect, the more modern sort. Perhaps I look forward most to the spectacle at the municipal stadium entitled: 'Ça ira, ça ira', wondering whether they will have Piaf's version of the rousing song. Certainly, if a guillotine is erected in the village afterwards, I won't have to take to the hills.

There are two chiming clocks in the village. One, on the town hall, is exact, but the one on the church is a few minutes late, and we call it the Tardy Clock. It's hard to say which the timetable will keep to. Maybe the Tardy Clock is the one by which tidings of the Revolution came, for it took over a week for the news to arrive from Paris.

But when it got there, things started to move. To be living at that time must have been heady indeed, until the price of bread started to go up. But now the price of bread is steady, and King Lotto is on the throne, though he will be mostly in the back seat when the celebrations begin in earnest, and a faint smile appears on Liberty's charming face.

The Retreat from Mons

In a village bar beyond St Quentin a well-built little girl in a long white dress and with a red ribbon in her hair said: 'Mama isn't in, at the moment. She's gone across the road to visit my grandmother, but she said she wouldn't be long. So, if you would like to sit down, you may wait.'

It was as formal and prepared a speech as I'd ever heard, all without taking the large dummy from her mouth, which undoubtedly added to her stance of self-assurance. She could have gone on for some time, but at that moment her mother came back, a pretty young blonde impossible not to chat with, while our table became littered with empty Orangina bottles the shape and size of hand grenades.

She was intrigued by our rucksacks, and I told her we were walking the route of the British Army's retreat from Mons in 1914 – or as much of it as we could. She probably thought we were barmy, but wished us *bon courage* as we went out of the door. What, in any case, was the Retreat from Mons? She must have wondered. Her grandmother had probably seen the khaki stream go through, the men asking for food and water. For me it was the last day of the stunt, of which more later.

When war was declared on 4 August 1914 the British expeditionary force of four infantry divisions and one cavalry division (eighty-one thousand men, thirty-two thousand horses, and several hundred guns) was shipped to France and detrained in the

Amiens-Le-Cateau area. More than half the men were reservists, many from sedentary occupations, called back to the colours only a few weeks before.

After two days on the march they formed a defence line east and west of the Mons-Condé canal. Immediately behind was the mining conurbation of the Borinage, whose houses, slag heaps and railway embankment gave good cover to a professional army that had learned much from its mistakes in the Boer War a dozen years before.

The battle took place on 23 August, and the British infantryman's aimed rifle-fire was rapid and deadly. 'Well entrenched and completely hidden,' the enemy account said, 'the British opened a murderous fire...the casualties increased...the rushes became shorter, and finally our whole advance stopped...with bloody losses.'

The novelist Walter Bloem, who was in the German ranks as a company commander, recalls: 'Our first battle is a heavy defeat, unheard of heavy defeat, and against the English, the English we laughed at.'

Nevertheless, it was the British who were defeated, because when two German Army corps sought to outflank them from the West a retreat was ordered for the following day, the infantry to be covered by General Allenby's cavalry division.

Such events were in my mind as I sat with Max Lehrain, my son-in-law, drinking beer in the *Grand Place* at Mons on a Sunday evening, high cloud echoing to firecrackers sounding like rifle shots. In the 1870s Verlaine spent two years in prison here for shooting at Rimbaud – and wrote some of his best poems.

Not from a slit trench, but the comfortable rooms at the Hotel Residence on 9 July, we walked at nine o'clock through an area reminiscent of the straggling towns of Nottinghamshire. Eighty thousand miners were until recently employed in the Borinage, and Van Gogh painted in one of its cottages, but the pit buildings were now derelict, headstocks quiescent and broken windows more numerous than those intact, which in any case were well grimed over.

The slag heaps from which the British soldiers dug in and fired on the advancing German regiments have been sown with pines, giving a rather dismal prospect to industry's honourable scars. Plain grass for pasture, or picnic spots, would have been better, though perhaps less able to resist the wind or hold rain.

The 1st Battalion of the Lincolnshire Regiment fought so hard the following day at Frameries that the enemy was in no condition to pursue, though they left forty of their own dead: 'Up to all the tricks of the trade from their experience of small wars,' a German writer said, 'the English veterans brilliantly understood how to slip off at the last moment.' They lay afterwards in a field to eat bully beef and biscuits, 'utterly tired out but undaunted', their faces blackened by smoke from bursting shells and their own rifle fire. Greatcoats and packs were left behind, as too burdensome to carry in the tropical heat.

At Eugenies a girl cycling by left a fragrant whiff of scented soap, we at the roadside feeding on bread and hard sausage, and a brew of tea from Max's stove. Two rusty German mortars decorated the gateway to a manor house.

Beyond sloping beet fields bordered by poppies lay the battlefield of Malplaquet, where the Duke of Marlborough defeated the French in 1709. 'A very murderous battle,' the Duke called it, thirty-two thousand men falling on the two sides, a fight almost barren of results in the ding-dong campaigns of that time. Ironically, the Lincolnshire Regiment had fought there as well.

Black-and-white cows were so big I expected them to be wearing horseshoes, one melancholy specimen looking at us disapprovingly through the bushes. The narrow lane to the frontier was paved with the same cobblestones that the troops found so trying to march on. A notice by the roadside, reminding cars to have papers, and pedestrians to carry passports, was passed without let or hindrance, and by two o'clock the first short stint of 24 kilometres brought us to Bavai in France.

A Dutch couple in the main square told us they were cycling to a festival of ethnic music near Orleans, and hoping to buy a set of bagpipes when they got there. The keys of the St Maur Hotel were attached to a large brass Star of David, and my first duty on getting to the room was to wash socks so that they would be dry by morning.

Bavai, a quiet old town off all main routes, was once the intersection of eight Roman roads, a place second only to Rheims in the towns of northern Gaul. When the Lincolnshires got there at the end of their day's march they slept in a deserted harvest field, and set out at 4.30 the following morning for Le Cateau.

We followed their tracks along the main road, careful to stay in to the left, eyes and ears open for traffic coming around the bends. Large dogs barked from every house. We bought bread in Le Quesnoy from a young woman who gave us a lovely smile. The town was fortified by Vauban, part of the seventeenth-century defence line across north-eastern France. When the New Zealanders retook it from the Germans in 1918 they scaled its walls with ladders, the last example of medieval warfare in Europe.

In rolling well-wooded country, high cloud held off the worst of the sun's heat. We took to narrow lanes leading through remote villages, bands of poppies bordering the road and cobblestones showing through a veneer of macadam. We politely refused a lift on an enormous lorry, which I don't suppose any of the soldiers would have turned down, had one been coming their way.

Our packs weighed about 20lb, not much hindrance in plodding up the long inclines between tall wheat ripe for the harvester: landscape little different from that of southern England, with patches of wood, a water tower, and the occasional steeple showing in the distance. At Salesches the map indicated a byway that had disappeared and, knocking on the nearest door to find out where it had gone, we were shown the right direction to the next village by an Englishwoman married to a Frenchman. She invited us in for coffee or tea, and though an acceptance would have made her happy, and us even more so, we had to turn it down in our hurry to reach Le Cateau, as if the Germans really were behind us.

We made coffee by a stream of ghastly effluent, though no factory was visible. Open wheat country marked the battlefield of

Le Cateau to our right, the same view as in 1914 except for a line of pylons crossing the defendable heights. The Lincolnshires were given ten minutes at the end of every hour, but were without food, and found very little water in the intense heat. Crowds of refugees were sidetracked from the roads, and a thunderstorm in the afternoon drenched everyone to the skin. At seven o'clock the battalion reached Inchy, a village bare of food. The next day they had fifty more casualties at the rearguard Battle of Le Cateau, fought after a drink of tea and a piece of bread each.

We descended towards Le Cateau by an unsignposted lane, and got there at five after walking 33 kilometres. Through a café window we spotted the *Guardian* photographer David Sillitoe, and made our rendezvous. The three of us lodged overnight at the Hotel Fénélon, which had excellent rooms and provided a good supper in its restaurant, not too close to the noisy main road.

I went to bed at ten, cutting off from the day by reading more of *The Aeneid* in a Penguin Classics edition. My feet were burning from blisters, socks soaked where they had burst, so that it was painful to walk, and not easy to look forward to the next day.

By early morning, after David had left for London on his motorbike with photographs, Max and I went marching on under a clear sky, a plastic container of water in each side pocket. The temperature was in the nineties, so I filled my army bottle as well. We took our first rest at a British military cemetery on the D12, most graves of men killed in 1918, when the enemy in their turn had been retreating.

We diverted for a short distance from the track of the Lincolnshire Regiment, but were still on the path of the main army, falling back towards the south-east of Paris on a wide band of parallel routes. The regimental history of the Lincolnshires records that on this day the troops were nearly worn out, but that morally their spirit was unbroken. By nightfall they had found water, but still no food.

At midday we made tea in a car park at Bohain, grateful for its canopy of trees. Thereafter the road was straight, the monotony broken only when a police car came level, its driver telling us to walk closer to the side of the road. We ate little, apart from bread and cheese, but drank all manner of liquids – water, tea, coffee and the ubiquitous but delicious cold Orangina. How the soldiers managed, I'll never know.

After 34 kilometres in the scorching sun we stopped for a drink before going on to the Hotel de la Paix at the southern end of St Quentin. My feet were burning from a coverage of more blisters, socks soaked again where some had burst. On peeling them off I plied a hot needle to pop the rest of them, then powdered the soles of my feet, but even so I could hardly stand up, and supposed that, had I been a soldier in 1914, I would either have become a prisoner of war, or been put on a regimental cart till their condition improved.

Through the pain came anger at my feet behaving so badly. I'd done similar walks but they'd never deteriorated to this extent. Maybe they were becoming like Admiral Nelson's stomach, which put him through a period of awful seasickness whenever he took to the ocean. I didn't see how I could walk any more, unless perhaps to the railway station across the river, without lying up for three days. Even stretched out in bed my feet burned and throbbed and I didn't see how I could put them down again.

Max, who had only minor lesions, went out to buy alcohol and plasters, and after a soaking and then covering all sore parts I decided to try the next day's lap of 23 kilometres, a quiet route along the wooded banks on the Somme as far as Ham.

We had the lanes to ourselves, and walked side by side, chatting on topics military and literary, and even singing occasionally. To go miles without seeing a car was heaven, except for my feet, for after a stop to make tea and have something to eat, it took ten minutes to get back to a normal walking rate, my crippled gait mocked by a lark singing above the sunken lane.

A large water tower stayed for hours in front, and then we seemed to have lost it behind the distant prospect of a ridge beyond Tugny. Away to the right a line of trees marked the main road from St Quentin, angling towards Ham, a few miles away.

Thought processes were reduced to nothing more than wondering when we were going to eat or rest or drink, or when we would pass the next landmark, each of great interest, whether man-made or not, in that soon it would be reached and left behind.

The last place before Ham was the hamlet of Estouilly, where the Lincolnshires halted on the morning of 28 August after an all-night march. They found the inhabitants enthusiastically digging trenches against the Germans, work that the troops took over. A foraging party into Ham came back with one tin of biscuits and a dozen tins of bully beef. Shared morsel by morsel, they seemed to give everyone fresh energy.

Their march that day, of nearly twenty kilometres along the dead straight shadeless road, took them almost to Noyon. Straggling was more noticeable, and when many fell out exhausted or with sore feet, stores and ammunition were dumped to make space for them on the carts. The hero of the day was indefatigable Lance-Corporal Snelling, who beat out lively tunes such as 'Tipperary' on his drum to keep the men going. In the evening half the battalion was billeted in cottages, and food was waiting for them at last.

From Noyon they marched on, as did the rest of the army, for another seven days, going through some of the fairest country in France. A French writer recalled: 'The soldiers, phlegmatic and stolid, march without appearing to hurry themselves; their calm is in striking contrast to the refugees. They pass a night in the villages of the Ourq. It is a pacific invasion . . . as sportsmen who had just returned from a successful shoot, our brave English eat with good appetite, drink stolidly, and pay royally those who present their bills; departing at daybreak, silently like ghosts, on the whistle of the officer in charge.'

In sixteen days the Lincolnshire battalion had marched 237 miles and fought two battles, a retreat summed up by the official historian: 'On arrival, they were hastened forward by forced marches to the battle, confronted with greatly superior numbers of the most renowned army in Europe – condemned at the very onset to undergo the severest ordeal which can be imposed upon an army. They were short of food and sleep when they began their retreat, they continued it always short of food and sleep for thirteen days, and at the end of the retreat they were still an army, and a formidable army. They were never demoralised, for they rightly judged they had never been beaten.'

After a couple of days to recuperate they joined the French in an advance to the Aisne, this time outflanking the Germans, and forcing them to retreat. During the fighting at Ypres, in the autumn and the following spring, most of them became casualties, few surviving the war.

Meanwhile, what was happening to the straggler at Ham, who had managed less than 80 miles? I avoided leaving technicoloured footmarks across the hotel floor by throwing down our old shirts to use as stepping stones to the bathroom, but the indication that the end of the march for me was at hand could not be ignored. We decided on a rest day, and next morning I called at the local hospital to get my feet dressed, though still with the hope of going on next morning.

The much-amused doctor asked how many more of us were doing such a crazy stunt. 'Just us two,' I had to tell him. After a close look at my feet he told me I needed to stay five days in the hospital for them to recover, implying that it would be foolhardy, perhaps even risky, not to do so. I felt tempted to take his advice, such smiling nurses having come in to see me as I lay on the table, but finally told them I would get on the train to Paris in the morning, and rest a day or two in a friend's flat. The nurse who dressed my feet so increased their size by the swathe of bandages that it looked as if I was suffering from gout. She fitted me with a pair of canvas green overshoes, and tied the strings around my legs, everyone agreeing that they went well with my khaki Rohan trousers.

I went into a small office at the end of the corridor to pay my bill, but the clerk, after half-filling in several forms, couldn't make up his mind what category to put me in, till the doctor and nurses together finally told him to throw the bill away. I went out to a taxi after heartfelt thanks for their skill and kindness. A year later, on my way south by car, I called in with presents for them all.

One man, as Max said, went to Meaux, and he walked on for nearly a hundred more miles during the next two days. I lightened his pack by taking a plastic bag of non-essentials, but he nevertheless deserved the Mons Star on proving that the march would still be done.

July 1990

Robbed!

At the end of 1813, after the Battle of Vitoria, the Duke of Wellington led his triumphant army over the Pyrenees into France. Among these Allied troops were Spanish units which, upon entering what they considered enemy territory, immediately spread out on an orgy of looting. Wellington had them rounded up and hanged a score or so, to demonstrate that no one in his army was allowed to behave in such a way.

When our car was looted in the town of Figueras a similar example could not be made, and in any case the thief, or thieves, were not caught. Nor will they be, but the decision as to whether or not they'd be hanged if they were, should it be left to me, would be a very close-run thing. Yet the affair was far less simple than in my anger I had thought at the time.

We had not particularly wanted to go into Spain, being holed up and working well in our house in Languedoc, but Ruth's American visa was running out, and the three months' limit on keeping the car in France had almost expired, so it was necessary to go over an international frontier, get our passports stamped to prove we had done so, then be free to come back. At the same time we decided to stay a night or two, have a look at the Costa Brava, and visit the Salvador Dali Museum in Figueras. Neither of us had been in Spain for twenty years, and it would be interesting to see how the country had changed since the death of Franco.

Instead of a quick run on the motorway and into Spain by Perthuis we decided to fork off at Perpignan and take the hilly coastal route by Port Bou, where we knew the scenery to be magnificent.

It was hard driving, along a twisting and crowded road, but the diversion was worth it. Arid and wooded hills flanked deep indentations showing the calm blue sea. The frontier post beyond the last French town seemed rather basic and relaxed, and we were out of France almost before realising until, remembering our purpose, I switched off the engine when the Spanish policeman made as if to wave us through. We asked in Spanish – not very rusty after so long a time – if he would stamp our passports. He performed the ritual reluctantly, as if he were there to watch but not to work. Our insistence prompted him to ask where we were going – in a casual enough manner between stamping one passport and the next. Without thinking, since we weren't sure where we would spend the night, I said we were on our way to Figueras.

After I had started the car Ruth commented that though we might indeed end up at that place we were not on the direct road to it, and that if we had intended to be we would have crossed the frontier by the motorway some distance to the West. It was only later, when we were back in France, that we heard on the news that the police of both countries had been especially vigilant that day, watching for people moving large amounts of 'laundered money' connected with the drug trade over the less usual frontier crossings.

We idled along the truly spectacular coast, which more than lived up to its name of Costa Brava, and in early evening headed west to Figueras. Next morning we paid our bill at the Hotel Trave and drove out of the garage. We later put the car in a large open public place near the centre of town, careful to lock every door and cover our possessions, then spent a couple of hours at the nearby Dali Museum. Fortunately I carried money, passports and car papers in my haversack.

When we got back to the car about midday we noticed the corner of a dress showing out of the closed overnight suitcase, which was uncharacteristic, but nothing was thought about it and we went off to continue our exploration of the coast.

It was a tiring day, and by half-past three we were booking into a quiet hotel at Cadaques. While sorting our luggage in the car park, deciding what to take to the room, I noticed that my brown Samsonite travelling bag was missing. Another overnight bag had things spilling out. The dress that had been showing from the suitcase was thus explained.

We cancelled our hotel room and, on the way back to report the robbery to the Policia Nacional at Figueras, went through the litany, as far as we were able, of what had been purloined, which included a Nikon camera, a pair of Kelvin Hughes binoculars with a built-in prismatic compass, and the Montblanc fountain pen with which I had written my novels over the last twenty years. They had also taken a notebook, my diary, a spare pair of glasses, and our two address books from an open bag.

I had been robbed once before in Spain, in Malaga in 1953, when my furnished room was ransacked and I lost everything, including money. On the present occasion we reflected that the entrance fee for the Dali Museum had cost us – considering what we spent on the trip, and the amount that would be necessary to replace all that was stolen – about £500 each. Maybe Dali would have been amused.

We stood at the counter of the police station, and were asked for our passports by a smart young officer who took down our *denuncio* in triplicate on a typewriter, which had to include my parents' first names. Perhaps he was so efficient and cool because he dealt with many such cases. At times during the tourist season there might even have been a queue. The list we gave was a long one, but even so we continued to recall other items only when we were driving back into France.

I was not unfamiliar with the inside of Spanish police stations. Reporting the robbery in Malaga, the police there could hardly be bothered to listen, the place full of shouting people who had also been plundered that same day, I was told, by one indignant supplicant. I was once taken to another police station against my will, in Barcelona in the fifties. I never knew on what charge, though I might have been opening my mouth a bit too wide about Franco on the overnight train from Madrid, and someone denounced *me*. I was released five hours later, but minus my French 'Carte d'Identité', which I was quite attached to in those days.

Here in Figueras all was polite and peaceful, so much so that none of the policemen on duty went out into the street to check our statement that the car door had been opened by someone using an almost duplicate key. The lock was hardly damaged, and could still be used.

The only purpose in reporting the robbery was to try and get something back through the insurance, though the time was wasted because this was the one occasion when we were not insured. We had found that there were problems travelling by car – in Spain, or anywhere else – because when you are between hotels, what are you to do with those objects not immediately needed and which you are reluctant to carry with you because, collectively, they are no mean weight?

Back in the street, it was after six in the evening, so we decided to return to France. We only stopped once before the frontier – using the direct road – to buy flowerpots with the money that would have been spent on the second night's hotel. Once on the motorway I put the car into overdrive, and in three hours we were home.

Several things occurred to us as we talked the matter over. It seemed strange that such items as a diary, a notebook, and the two address books had been taken. They hadn't been scooped up by accident at the joy of so rich a haul, but deliberately chosen from many other objects. I was as intrigued and even worried by this as by what else was missing. Even if my notebook etc. had been in the bag with the binoculars, they had extracted the others from a container that had nothing else missing from it.

Such things were valueless to any ordinary thief, who would have left them where they were. It was also obvious that the car had been gone through at comparative leisure, so maybe someone had followed us to the Dali Museum before the exercise began. This and the blasé attitude of the police – though to give them credit they voiced regrets at the end of the *denuncio* that our

121

holiday had been spoiled – leads me to wonder whether they already knew, even before we appeared to report it, that our car had been rifled.

It was certainly a very skilful break-in, and seemed done mainly to get at our address books and any other papers. If this was so, the thief had, of course, to take everything of value so as not to arouse suspicions, such goods also no doubt paying him for his trouble.

When we came through the frontier we had very little in the car, apart from a few cardboard boxes of camping equipment, which we had not bothered to take out after our trip to England. If the car had been occupied by a harassed couple and three fractious children, with all their holiday-making appurtenances, cases on the luggage rack held down by a flapping sheet of plastic, maybe we wouldn't have been so marked out. In fact I think that those wishing to take huge amounts of laundered drug money – or any other illegal merchandise – over the frontier, would have kitted themselves out in just such a manner. The Rent-a-Kid Company Limited must do a fair amount of business that way.

So what did the Drug Bureau of Spanish Interpol think when they had our things laid out on a table before them? The compass-binoculars were certainly suspect. You could look out to sea and read off the magnetic bearings of any approaching smugglers' boat. In my notebook were copies of the Greek, Russian and Hebrew scripts, as well as various navigation and map-reading conversion formulae, and the radio frequencies of W/T weather stations in the Channel and the North Sea. As for our address books, I imagine they are pondering over them yet, because most of the entries were of publishers, newspaper editors, literary magazines, and my agent – the perfect address books, perhaps, of a smuggler about to retire and hoping to sell his memoirs.

All we wanted was to get our passports stamped, and show evidence that I had taken the car out of France within three months, but when we got back to the Languedoc someone told us that such a procedure wasn't necessary anymore, that with the advent of the full Common Market Regulations we needn't have bothered. Thank you very much.

So now, may I ask the Spanish branch of Interpol, or whatever they call themselves, to at least kindly return our address books? We are lost, and will not be able to contact a great many friends without them. I would also like to see my notebook, which contained ideas for several stories – tales of fiction, however, unlike the one just told.

Guardian *Diary Piece*

Cruising at ninety on the motorway towards Genoa, the left front wheel seems to rattle over a bunch of steel rods. I'm on my way from our house near Montpellier in France to the International Poetry Festival at Struga, on the Albanian border with Yugoslavia. For a moment there seems no doubt as to whether or not I'll get there, but a week is allowed for the sixteen hundred miles, including stopovers and calling in on friends. Three more weeks for the return will mean a beneficial month from the middle of a novel. There is no better way to get clear of such bondage than to take to the steering wheel and see landscapes.

The noise persists so, puncture or not, I daren't immediately stop, but allow the sturdy old Peugeot Estate to manoeuvre itself into the inner lane. No sign of a layby, another tunnel is coming up, so many along this coast that much of the way seems to be underground, glimpses of sea and sky mostly spent overtaking lorries and slow coaches.

The car bumps ominously on the wheel rim, but at the end of the tunnel there's a place to stop, and I get in gently. It must be about 140 degrees in the sun but the spare wheel is soon unlocked and the car jacked up. The nuts don't come loose till each one is forcefully kicked by my boots, and then they do. Sweat splashes onto the gravel. A man walks off the motorway holding my hub plate. How he recovered it, I'll never know. He wears a tie and a good suit, and mentions a Michelin depot in a village just north of Genoa. The tyre is almost shredded, and too hot to touch. He takes over the work, and fixes the wheel back in place. I offer him a cigar, but he doesn't smoke. I wonder what he is doing in the layby, since my car is the only one there. He says he has an appointment for someone to pick him up in half an hour. An assignment with his girlfriend, perhaps? I drive off and leave him in a state of tense expectation.

A German family takes a table and four chairs from their caravan and brings out plates and cutlery for dinner. I am in a large service-station area near Verona. After a 400-mile day I decided it was time to get off the motorway and look for a hotel. An hour of searching provided nothing, the southern shore of Lake Garda in August no place to find a night's lodging. I felt as scruffy and exhausted as after a day's work in the factory, and must have looked it too, judging by the reaction of clerks and well-groomed people going by on their way to dinner. There was not a room to be had, so I decide to sleep in the car, whose front seats fold back to form a bed.

I open the tailgate and clear enough space to set up a small stove and make tea. Delicious food smells come from the German caravan, but I've already had an indifferent supper in the restaurant. I drink tea in the front seat and by the light of a torch lose myself in a few more pages of Clive Sinclair's new novel *Cosmetic Effects*.

Strolling around the area before sleep time I note the German family getting themselves into position for supper: father, mother, a girl of about five and a large Alsatian dog, which takes its place on the fourth chair. They're a merry lot, though they don't give any wine to the dog, which looks a fierce and sullen brute as it chomps into its commons. I move my car fifty yards further into the dark in case it gets loose during the night.

Ten miles short of Zagreb a traffic hold-up goes far into the distance, and gives no sign of moving, so I turn the car and set off into the byways, hoping to find a way to the autoroute, which leaves for Belgrade to the south of the city. Apart from the Michelin map I have a sheet of the area printed by the Royal Engineers, which is slightly more detailed. Making several unsuccessful forays up leafy lanes and into the dead-ends of farmyards, I get myself on and spot, after a few more miles, the rise of the motorway ahead. In my rear mirror I notice half a dozen German cars whose drivers have followed my trail, thinking me to be familiar with the area. They were lucky, but so was I, while appreciating their waves as we all head into freedom.

The motorway gives out and becomes the same Arterial Ribbon of Death I negotiated on the way to Israel in 1977. The opposite lane is crowded with holiday traffic coming back to Western Europe. A car on the empty side in front, temporarily in the distance seems no threat, until I realise it is coming my way and head on, overtaking at the price of his life and mine.

This happens many times, but the technique is to slow down quickly and get far into the verge so that the other car can whisker by, which is always the case. One doesn't even curse, since it's not every day one has the privilege of facing annihilation and living to tell the tale.

On the relative safety of the motorway again the tailgate springs open and the two straw hats are sucked out, but it's safer not to stop and chase them.

We are in the motel at Titograd (it used to be called Podgorica, and soon will be again). The Festival of Struga ended a couple of days ago. No more miles of poetry small-talk among scenery that deserved better. On my arrival there I drove to the airport (a glorified landing strip) and waited to meet Ruth Fainlight coming in on the plane from London. The rendezvous worked, though at times on my long haul from Montpellier it had seemed a very long shot indeed. The pilot brought the plane gliding in, a perfect landing, and so I was also able to give a lift into town to Elaine Feinstein and her husband Arnold.

After our last reading in Skopje we skirted the Albanian border, a slow drive in rain along a narrow road beset with car traffic and heavy lorries. The 200 miles through the tortuous mountain ranges of Montenegro seemed long ones, but at least we are sitting down to a decent meal and the usual half-litre of red. On entering Jugoslavia ten days ago the exchange rate had been 40,000 dinars to the pound, and now it is 47,000 – a horrifying speed of inflation, from which God preserve us. Nevertheless, we begin to feel ourselves founder members of the Dinar's Club.

In the morning I see that someone has wrenched off the right-hand wing mirror of my car. In Russia of the sixties it was necessary to unscrew all exterior appurtenances, even when the car was guarded at night. You took them into your hotel room, but wing mirrors on the newer Peugeots can't be unscrewed any more. To report the damage to the nearby militia post would mean facing delays, to no purpose. Perhaps some partisan who doesn't know the war is over came out of the hills and wanted to see what he or she looked like after so long a time. Or maybe they communicate by heliograph in these parts – when the rain stops.

The road out of Podgorica (as I'll call it) goes along high ground north of Lake Scutari in Albania, a milky mist along its surface in the distance. Joyce Cary was in these parts during the war against the Turks in 1911–12, working as a medical orderly, after leaving university. He followed the Montenegrin advance along the shores of the lake ('In the Land of the Bobotes') with his own charming illustrations.

We stopped an hour in Cetinje, the old capital of Montenegro, a peaceful town of wide streets and mostly low houses. Baedeker says that, 'In some respects the place resembles a little German country town, but it has several distinctive features of its own.' Pretty girls walk arm in arm along the main street, and the men indeed were 'remarkably dignified in their bearing', though no longer carried 'an arsenal of weapons in their girdles'.

Our guidebooks for the trip are Baedeker's *Austria, 1896*, and the latest *Guide Bleu*, a combination that still makes some kind of sense, especially about Dubrovnik, or Ragusa, where we put up at the Imperial Hotel. The room gives a wide view over the walled city and out to sea, but the decibel rate of traffic noise is shattering by day and night. Therefore we leave next day, though 24 hours are barely enough to sample the baroque beauties of that Adriatic city.

I reflect on our way up the spectacular coast that, with a car like this, one could spend weeks exploring the lesser-known parts of Yugoslavia, the disparate entities of an endlessly fascinating country. Detailed maps are difficult to get, except for the littoral, but that would only make the trip more interesting.

At the entrance to every town people approach to ask if you want a room for the night in their house or flat, which is cheaper than going to a hotel. We risk it in Split, to have the experience, and for three £5 notes get a small and noisy room, with continental breakfast for two. After dark we go to the middle of town to eat, and only find our way back to the block of flats because I had bought a detailed map from a bookstall. Next morning in the cramped flat I end up making coffee and tea from our own supplies in the car, but we're satisfied with our cheap night-stop, and the people were pleasant.

A traffic hold-up along the coast can't be bypassed this time, due to mountainous terrain. Two hundred yards in front a Jugoslav and a German car have collided, children's toys scattered over the asphalt, dead and injured being cut free. It's like a battlefield, I muse, which is maybe why one doesn't travel by rail. At Zadar (or Zara) we take the boat across the Adriatic for Ancona, since we had planned it that way – still a great distance from home, but with all the enjoyment of being on the road.

Up the Rigi

The necessity of buying a watch in Switzerland (the spring on my own had broken soon after landing) was an even more felicitous inconvenience than having an electronic calculator go phut in Taiwan. The train seemed to be a minute late on leaving Zurich, but it was only because the new watch hadn't been set correctly. To synchronise it by the train's departure may not qualify as chronometer standard, but it would no doubt have been accurate enough for longitude to save Sir Cloudsley Shovel's fleet from disaster at the Scillies in 1707.

On the spare half-hour in Zurich I went window shopping along the nearby Bahnhof Strasse, and saw a hugely wing-spanned white swan sweeping gracefully down the length of it just above the traffic.

On the ascent through gullies and woods and meadows from Goldau the needle of my pocket altimeter moved around its dial as the rack-and-pinion train squeaked and rattled ever upwards, till soporific air near the summit sent the eyelids pressing towards closure. Alighting below the Rigi Kulm Hotel all I wanted to do, therefore, was sleep. Talks and readings in Zurich, Berne and Basel (which a writer must do to earn his keep, make himself known, but above all to pay for foreign travel) called for a rest, though it was only midday.

A nun carrying a rucksack, black headdress flowing in the wind, made her way down the paved track as I went towards the

129

hotel with my shoulder bag, having taken Baedeker's advice, which no traveller can fault: 'A superabundance of luggage infallibly increases the delays, annoyances, and expense of travel.'

Several American families meandered around the large space before the hotel, contemplating the odd blob of snow, then grouped at a kiosk to choose postcards. A father cautioned his five-year-old son, quite rightly, against running down the steep slope, in case he fell over a cliff and vanished as in an Edward Gorey narrative.

The Alps, streaked and capped with white, demanded to be looked at through binoculars, so that even from this distance their snow seemed to draw the body into it, burrowing till cold became warm and you didn't wake up. So I put the glasses back into their case, to see the whole 125-mile range from the vantage point of 6,000 feet.

I'd had a quiet lunch in the hotel on the way back from Israel four years ago, but today looked like the busiest time of the year. An overworked waiter gave me the key to a second-storey room with two beds. The floor was wooden, but runner carpets by the bedsides cushioned the feet, otherwise it was bare wood, except in the tiled bathroom. A chest of drawers, two chairs and an armchair, a wardrobe, and an oval table to write at, should the mood come, or to spread a map on before setting out for a walk in fine weather – should that come too – completed the simple oldish-style furniture.

A snack in the crowded restaurant would do, I thought, before picking up the menu and seeing the good things written about. It was Sunday, and also Mother's Day, when all the good women of Switzerland were taken out for a meal, which might have been why every table had a vase of flowers or a potted plant set on it. Some mothers had been brought by their children, the rule being that on such a day she shall not cook or wash up or sew or go rub-a-dub-dub at the wash tub, or even flick on the switch of a shining white machine, but must be taken out and made to feel even more of a queen than she had always known herself to be. If her children no longer lived at home they must go back with flowers and chocolates, and persuade her (who was all dressed up and waiting) to come out for a day's excursion. Yet a few old couples must have had children who were either dead or lived too far away – in Tasmania or Alaska – to come and take them out. Or rebellious offspring had discarded both custom and conscience, in which category a group of young people dining jovially in the corner might well have fitted.

A glasss-fronted bookcase (no doubt locked; I didn't try it) contained the works in homogenous leather bindings of German and Swiss authors from the previous century, so many volumes as to have taken at least one cow from its pristine pasture. In a wooden frame to the left were printed the times of the year's sunrises, while to the right an identical frame gave details of the sunsets, said to be the same that Mark Twain had looked at during his stay, and described in *A Tramp Abroad*. A couple of elk heads on the facing wall were kept company by a wooden crucifix, which gave them little comfort.

I succumbed to a meal of soup, a plate of asparagus (it being May, so in season) and a main course of veal and spaghetti. The remaining half-portion warming in a platter by the table had to be resisted if my appetite was to cope with the mountain range of ice-cream, demi-strawberries pressed into it as if to flagmark the places where climbers had come to grief. The need for sleep then pressed more weightily but, on going outside, the Alps were too much in view, even at this distance radiating enough energised electricity to keep me from a comfortable bed. I went downhill with alacrity, a clack of boots on the paved track, pressure behind the legs and across the toes as the strain was taken, speed a necessity since it was difficult not to run on a slope more suitable for goats. In the train from Zurich a jacket had been too heavy, but a sweater had to be put on around the summit of the Rigi.

The noise of Mother's Day faded and, alone in meadows speckled with cowslips, crocuses and gentians – no green so rich and juicy-looking as that of an alpine meadow – I could sing, stand on my head, talk to myself, mutter against whatever malign fate might have in store, or crawl on hands and knees like the demented poet Lenz on that twentieth day of January as he made his way through the mountains, as told in Georg Buchner's story.

At the Rigi-Staffel station a muddy and snow-blotched path forked to the Belvedere at First, though first I went to the trigonometrical point at 1,797.5 metres marked on the attractive Swiss map impossible to open in the wind, or refer to the pull-out panorama in my old Baedeker. Spinning away in tatters over the crags and bushes, they would have been lost forever.

Returning to the hotel meant pushing against a gale, a labour of step by step like an old man, though a youth ahead went slowly enough. One certainly had cause to wonder why mountains were so configured that air currents were always against you, the wind now howling like an indignant cat as if a young boy gleefully pulled its tail and wouldn't let go.

After tea I fell asleep, miles from the nearest internal combustion engine, not even noise from the crowded hotel; reaching my dreams, but woken eventually by the whine and thump of a departing train, I went downstairs to find few people left on the premises. All of the waiters and waitresses, and some elderly women, were washing up together, with no sign of demarcation disputes.

From the highest trig point the sun was seen going down towards France as if never to come back. But the sun was as regular as sin, and surely would, otherwise how could it have been worshipped so assiduously by the Ancients? The wind played a comb-and-paper tune on a nearby railing, and the half-inch ash from my cigar vanished like grey dust.

The orange sphere, melting into a turquoise sky through different bands of colour, seemed at rest for a while, as if reluctant to leave the Rigi to its darkness, but the whole line of the Alps was slowly disappearing, the sun's bonfire on the horizon discarding a plume of flame, a vermillion afterglow pointing south.

Hotels in which you feel yourself a guest of the family are rare, though many give that impression in Switzerland. As the only overnight lodger, a specially typed menu lay on my table at supper: 'NACHTESSEN: Gemusecremesuppe', was followed by

132

'Schweinshaxe "Fruhlingsart", Lyonskartoffeln, Rotkraut,' completed by 'Coupe Jacques'.

More than three days (and I would stay for as many months) in the peace that, while it did not pass understanding, would enable me to write a novel, and forget the entanglements of modern life – before descending to face it again. All that was needed in my refuge of a room was a change of clothes, a few books and a typewriter. Prokofiev's 'Cendrillon' played softly on the radio, needling, jerky, blood-irritant, gadfly music when not sugary and too sweet, so I switched it off.

In a folder of envelopes and notepaper was a card with the name and address and telephone number of a 'Spezialarzt FMH Für Psychiatre und Psychotherapie'. Maybe people do go mad in such solitude, or were so before arrival, but in the eighteenth century Lenz had to seek out a benign minister of religion to pacify his soul. Had he been living today and stumbled into the Hotel Rigi-Kulm (and maybe any other such place in the Alps), he could have had treatment on the premises.

I decided to make a Sabbath of my seventh morning in Switzerland and stay an extra hour in bed, but woke at six to see a silk white mist blocking the view from both windows: the wind had stopped moaning, not a good sign for seeing the famous dawn over the Alps. Drifting back into divine rest, only dreams proved I was still alive (since in death there can be none), the bed my womb till a late rising at eight o'clock. A gentle wind might clear the mist, bringing rain, then more mist, so I was happy to do nothing, since a walk would call for navigation by compass and dead-reckoning to avoid falling over a cliff. In any case I had already seen the whole range, picked out the Eiger and the Jungfrau.

Bird noises indicated clearer weather, but by breakfast snow was falling. When it stopped, visibility improved. Then it closed in again. Pellets of snow blew horizontally on my walk to the trig point, a matter of forty metres in height and a few hundred yards distance. An elongated three-sided figure made out of steel was supported on four legs and came to a point sharp enough to pierce a shrike that inadvertently alighted on it. In the hotel bar –

as large as the dining room – twelve plywood lampshades were modelled on the same trig figure.

A group of English tourists in anoraks and plastic hoods stood before the hotel; one, I thought, to be a man in hiking garb of about forty, with rugged features, till she turned with a smile to her husband. The young man guiding the party was giving a dissertation on Japanese cinema, his listeners impressed with his knowledge one moment and bored the next. The pink-faced husband of the mannish woman was as much interested in the cicerone's snow-white teeth as anything, so maybe he was a dentist. Perhaps his wife was, as well – my assumptions spiralling off as usual into an infinity of speculations as to their private life. They had come up from the lowlands for a glimpse of the mountains, but showed no disappointment on walking to catch a train from a stop lower down: they had seen the future, and it snowed.

Sleep, eat and walk was the rule, so I plodded a thousand feet down to where the mist floated across the meadows of flowers, bird sounds dominated by the lunatic insistence of the cuckoo, plus a tinkle of bells from invisible cows. A few rays of sun showed the opaque water of Lake Zug, sprouting its fjords, soon gone, then displayed again, the wind a film director playing his cloud machine.

Smoking an after-supper cigar at the window, the line of the Alps seemed as if especially laid out, no cloud between. After heavy night-time snow, shoulders and knolls jutted from licks of pure whiteness, showing brown peaks and escarpments, a broken symmetry no artist would have the patience and ingenuity to construct. The complete view from an aeroplane gave a slow-moving photograph, magnificent in its way, but now in the evening and from this angle and distance, with a blue sky above and shreds of cloud advancing along the tops to leave most peaks visible, it was plain that I hadn't come here for nothing. Flaubert complained in 1874 that he found the Rigi dull, and would 'swap all the glaciers of Switzerland for the museum in the Vatican', but to me there is a place and a time for everything, so why not have both?

All bits and pieces in my haversack, I paid the bill, and went to a station lower down the mountain to meet my publisher and his wife, who wanted a day out of Zurich to do a few hours' walking. Heavy machine-gun fire came from an army range near Kussnacht, a village at whose inn Goethe had stayed in 1797; but in Europe over the centuries there was always someone who had stayed somewhere, celebrities ever travelling by coach, boat or on shanks's pony.

At the station a man was digging and scraping with a pick to tidy out a channel along the opposite platform. Visibility increased and decreased, yet it finally cleared and seemed set fair for the next few days as the train drew in and my friends stepped from their carriage.

Incomparable Derbyshire

A landscape is only memorable when signs of human life are combined with a visual grandeur that seems to have come about by the growing pains of an infant earth that had no Doctor Spock to control its geological tantrums. Derbyshire has such characteristics, and Byron said there are things in that county 'as noble as in Greece or Switzerland'. While poets exaggerate in order to hear themselves talk when they think no one else might listen (though often more loudly knowing they will, much like everyone else), it's hard not to endorse his opinion.

For me, Derbyshire begins at that ribbon of resorts in the winding Derwent Valley known as Matlock, and I drove there at the beginning of April, randomly selecting the Temple Hotel for a night's lodging. Queen Victoria stayed there when it was an annex to the New Bath Hotel, and Byron left his mark – when did he not? – by scratching a poem on the window pane. A large room with a shower, toilet and four-poster bed cost a reasonable £20, while an evening meal added £5 more.

After a sumptuous English breakfast (often my favourite meal of the day), I went outside to find that my car wouldn't start, due to a freezing all-night mist, so I set off to climb the Heights of Abraham, hoping it would miraculously mend itself in the meantime.

Paying 60p to get into the area, I followed a track through woods to the viewing platform. On the way, a little offside among the trees, stands a small log lean-to as if built for poet or sibyl to sit in and be inspired by the isolation or, if she can, to watch people panting up the hill.

The door to the tower was open – a rare welcome – and stone steps led to the viewing platform, muted traffic heard from 800 feet below. Ridges and hilltops came into sunlit view, through gaps in heavy mist still hanging over the valley. A cable-car system connects with the opposite hill and, just below the tower, beside the green-and-yellow Swiss-style railway station, three tiny cars were threaded onto the cable, each with a bulbous glass window at the front. Bluebottle heads hanging on the wires, one behind the other, like the result of some ferocious decapitation done as a warning to others.

Olive greensward sloped up to Masson Hill, bits of crestline to the South sticking up like an old sailor's teeth ruined by years of hardtack, making the area seem grand and precipitous, though the hill behind was barely 1,200 feet. Clusters of houses became visible on the hillside, and a hole in the mist showed a bus going along the main road.

Four miles south-east, beyond the neighbouring Heights of Jacob (the old Derbyshire folk were nothing if not biblical), Crich Tower stood on a shelf of cloud like a rocket ready to blast off into blue space, as if Derbyshire had secretly prepared a space programme and was now ready to astonish the world – though it is, as every entrance to the country testifies, a 'nuclear free zone'.

The Tower is a monument erected 'In Memory of 11,409 men of all ranks of the Sherwood Foresters (Nottinghamshire and Derby Regiment) who gave their lives for King and Country in the Great War of 1914–1919.' Both countries from which the dead men came were visible, an enormous patch of dark wood on the Derbyshire side shaped like the horseshoe of the Carpathians on a layered map, while on the opposite skyline were the colliery villages of Nottinghamshire, most no longer working.

Matlock was started on its career as a spa by John Smedley, a nineteenth-century hosiery manufacturer, whose health had broken down due to worry and overwork. Scorning doctors' remedies, he built a series of opulent 'hydros' at which people could be healed by cold water. The Romans were drawn to Matlock because of its lead mines, but for a hundred or more years excursionists have come from the nearby industrial cities to enjoy the scenery and pure air, and today Smedley's buildings have turned into offices, or are used for educational purposes.

A person of note who lived in the area has to be Phoebe Brown, the dextrous Amazon of Matlock Green, who, in her time – she died in 1854 at the age of 82 – defended herself in that masculine era with her fists, and with weapons made at her blacksmith's forge. She was also a carpenter and mason, could walk forty miles a day, and do any kind of labour, which included breaking in horses at a guinea each. She also read Milton, Pope and Shakespeare, and played the flute, violin or harpsichord in church.

Back at the hotel, the car still not sparking into life, I sat on the terrace in the sun and drank coffee till the RAC man came in his van, gave the battery a jolt, and set me back on the road.

Chatsworth, home of the eleventh Duke of Devonshire, is a grim-looking building ten miles north, but the grounds of bucolic, though man-made complexity are well worth seeing. For £2.75 I was permitted to walk around the great house and linger unescorted, the route cleverly arranged between roped-off areas and closed doors so that there is no chance of getting lost in its nearly two hundred rooms, or of disturbing the duke at lunch.

This 'Palace of the Peak' is full of sculpture and pictures, and deserves more than the hour that I gave to it. Paintings to stop all progress include Poussin's *Landscape with Setters*, *A View of Tivoli* – attributed to Salvatore Rosa – and Veronese's *Adoration of the Magi*. Opera glasses (something I always carry) brought the pleasing female flesh painted on the ceilings as close as if to be touched.

A notice in the library warned against handling the books, as if someone had seen me coming, such exquisitely bound volumes impossible to acquire on a writer's income. Views from the windows are almost as inspiring as those on the walls and tapestries within, rivulets and lawns falling away against a background of gentle hills. A tall, thin escalade of water comes down in a cloud of soft foam from the hillside, while other windows show ponds, fountains and delicate stone bridges.

After wandering around like the owner of the place you may buy maps and postcards in the shop, as well as cakes, pots of honey, earthenware vessels and ornamental trays. The establishment gives employment in running and upkeep, but still not enough money is made, which is a pity, because Andrew Devonshire, the present duke, may have to auction 74 old master drawings to cover the repair of leaking roofs, frayed carpets and deteriorating silk coverings.

Huge crows on fence posts north of Buxton survey the empty moors in every direction – no beauty here as in the landscape around Matlock, at least not until the valley of Edale comes into view from the Castleton road, where the grand circus of beige-coloured hills is broken by grey panellings of cliffs. In the fields newborn lambs totter after their ewes. For several miles the road winds by hamlets and farms, the valley seeming to be a cul-de-sac that only the working farmer and summer fell walker know about. The long-distance footpath of the Pennine Way starts here, ending after 250 miles at the Scottish frontier.

Walking was not always allowed in the area, the land kept wild and free for grouse, but in 1932 four hundred people met for a mass trespass on the wide tableland of Kinder Scout. Newsreels of the time make the foray look like troops going over the top in the Great War, but the ramblers were advancing against police and gamekeepers, and five of the so-called ringleaders ended up in prison. The Pennine Way was opened in 1965, though free access to the moors is still forbidden.

The way to Eyam, rhyming with 'stream', leads through a wooden valley that indeed has a stream whose moving water glints between the trees. The switch from dramatic to subtle scenery comes with little expectation. Part of the road overhanging an escarpment has crumbled away, so only one car can pass at a time, and Eyam seems quite as cut off now as during the incidents of the Great Plague, which gave it fame ever after.

A man who opened a box of clothes sent from London in September 1665 infected the whole of his family, and before the end of the year 46 people were dead. Snow and frost then checked the disease, but it broke out again for an even worse killing spree. Some say that by the end of the outbreak only 30 inhabitants were left out of 350.

Many more might have perished in the plague-free area beyond the village if the Reverend Mompesson hadn't talked his parishioners into staying within the cordon he had drawn, beyond which no one was to stray. The outside world, happy at such an arrangement, left supplies of food at certain points along the boundary. Money for payment was placed in a shallow trough of running water (since known as 'Mompesson's Well') to cleanse it from infection.

Mompesson and his wife sent their children away before the blockade began. Seven died in one family, to be buried by the surviving mother. Mompesson's wife perished, but he lived another forty years. Every cottage in which people succumbed still has its plaque of notoriety, of which I felt myself a part.

According to all accounts, Mompesson had no easy task persuading people to remain in the infected area. The parson's word was law, however, though two men made a run for it, and got away, and I can only hope they were among the survivors.

An eerie aspect still lingers about the place, as I ghoulishly walked with map in hand, tramping the fields, and studying the gravestones, wondering if my name would be on any of them. Without the plague Eyam would have been no more than another attractive Derbyshire village.

Grey stone and green banks to either side of the winding lane took me south again. The car splashed through a ford, and went over open country to Tissington (famous for its 'well-dressing') till the jagged green shape of Thorpe Cloud Hill marked the beginning of Dovedale. What nature makes, man will praise, and Izaak Walton said much about the place in his *Compleat Angler*. Even Doctor Johnson, who preferred towns, and was shocked by Derbyshire's 'horrid hills', said: 'He that has seen Dovedale has no need to visit the Highlands of Scotland.'

A path goes for three miles up the glen, and you can take your picnic lunch to the packhorse bridge at Milldale, then walk back through scenery that makes those engravings in Victorian guidebooks seem realistic. In the enclosed glen the sight and sound of running water is always present, and gives a romantic and Gothic charm, some parts perfectly fitted for the playing of a doomed love affair, or dastardly crime. The last bear seen in England was said to have been killed near Dovedale.

An escarpment going to the sky ends at rags of grey cloud floating over. Dead trees are wreathed in anacondas of ivy, and winter catkins hang in isolation, but at the next curve of the path a woman is pushing a pram, and a geological hammer swings from her husband's belt.

A few score children's anoraks make a moving rainbow along the river, before they congregate at a stile. Outcrops, generally rectangular, look as if built of small bricks that have been crumbling for a hundred years. A splash of sunlight reflects trees and pinnacles in the water, giving a downward as well as upward view, while an enormous chisel-blade of rock seems poised to scrape the sky. On the way back the fields on a green hillside are divided by the faint letter L of a stone wall going to the summit. Above the wood individual trees are scattered as if held by soldiers advancing towards Macbeth's castle at Dunsinane.

Derbyshire, in the middle of England, and a fifty-mile stretch of country from the Vale of Trent to the High Peak, repays exploration. I can't recall the number of times I've done the tour, and though wouldn't liken it to Greece or Switzerland, the country is unique, and needs no comparisons.

On Joseph Conrad

In 1948 I was, for a few days, a wireless operator on a Royal Air Force pinnace, which was acting as radio link and dogsbody for a flotilla of naval vessels laying out a bombing range off the north-west coast of Malaya. Unlike near the mangrove swamps further south, there was no smell except that of the pure sea.

Even at dead of night the air was overpoweringly warm and, on anchor watch, the boat at rest in the bay of a jungle-covered island, I would periodically sling the lead to make sure there was no drift onto abrasive rocks nearby. I was tempted, as each counted minute passed, to lay down on the deck and fall criminally to sleep, so in order to resist I slung the lead more often than necessary, such irregular splashings not pleasing to those trying to sleep below.

My period of work on the pinnace – short as it was, for I was no sailor – led me to consider exchanging the wireless qualifications gained in the air force for those of a Marconi officer in the Merchant Marine, as soon as I was demobilised. Those high-funnelled rusting steamers seen in Penang harbour from our camp under the palm trees on the mainland had an aura of romance, and I could easily see myself occupying the wireless cabin on one of them, calling around the East Indies and along the China coast. Throughout my childhood I had swallowed wholesale the romance of Empire and now, with the Dutch being pushed from Batavia, and the beginning of the Malayan Emergency, that Empire was crumbling around me.

Fate decided that my dream of working on ships would not become reality. In Malaya, maps and charts had been my mainstay in forever fixing the position as to where I was and, in my work of shortwave direction finding, telling others by Morse where *they* were. Such continual preoccupations with the earth's surface held the clue to present and future wanderings, which fact seemed even more pertinent when I later read that classic of psychology and geography so poignantly matched in *The End of the Tether*. There was much about the Far East just after the Second World War that still gave off an atmosphere of Conrad's fiction, and reading his work not only brought places vividly to mind but moved me because I too was becoming a novelist.

The earliest known photograph of Conrad shows him holding a toy whip, and behind the child's expression of angelic mystery is a more subtle tone of pitiable disturbance. He seems already to have reached the end of his tether, a facial conflict suggesting that one half of himself will drive the other half from the village of Terechova, both to escape the torment in which he was born, and in an attempt to cure the anguish that impels him.

An ineradicable lust to move is formed before birth. People are congenitally influenced, but the tragic occurrences of Conrad's young life forced him to travel as far as possible from where he was born. This urge took him to places and into an occupation diametrically opposed to what he would become, as if he would devote his life to resisting such a fate. In the most extreme physical situations, as seaman and officer of sailing ships, he struggled all the more fiercely the closer he came to the destiny of turning into a writer.

According to Robert Graves it is necessary for a poet to die in his youth and be born again, if only symbolically, so as to then enter the positive phase of his vocation. Conrad attempted suicide in Marseilles early in 1878, and shortly afterwards obtained work on an English ship. After such a symbolic death and subsequent rebirth he was unable to deny the elemental force that had always been in him.

Conrad was born near Berdichev in 1857, and baptised in the Roman Catholic church in Zhitomir. No guidebook to Russia that

I have seen recalls his association with the area, perhaps because he was ideological poison to both the Tsarist and Soviet regimes. Travelling by car through Ukraine in the summer of 1967, I was prevented from driving into Berdichev by a militiaman, and made to go back to the bypass.

Carrying an old Austrian survey map, I had also noticed a place called Verkhovnya, 30 miles east of Conrad's birthplace. Anyone familiar with the life of Balzac will know that he not only spent the end of 1848 and the whole of 1849 there but was married at Berdichev to the 'noble and virtuous' Countess Eveline Hanska, after sixteen years of pursuit – because she was a married woman with five children and he had to wait for the husband to die.

Conrad came, of course, to know Balzac's work, and must have been aware of his familiarity with the district seven years before his own birth. Later in life he indicated that Balzac and Stendhal were authors he most admired. Though the guidebooks don't mention Conrad, the fact of Balzac's marriage was recorded by Chekhov when Chebutykin quotes that famous line from a newspaper in *The Three Sisters*, in order to deny that nothing ever happened in provincial Russia: 'Balzac was married in Berdichev.'

Heredity and circumstance mix, and it is often difficult to tell one influence from another, but the geography of the birthplace cements them together, such fusion creating the divine urge in the heart of a child to become a novelist.

Conrad, in his youth, was to put insuperable obstacles in his own path. Continual attempts to break out of a cul-de-sac, and the experience of being many times at the end of his tether, led him to choose the most distant yet congenial blind alley of the English language.

A message that the ending of youth hammers home is that life will not go on forever, and that a choice must be made by correctly divining and then accepting the course Fate has chosen with neither quibble nor reservation.

A novelist shapes lives, gives form to chaos, and hopes his characters will stay in the human imagination forever. To this end he uses them more outrageously than Fate ever can, so as to show his readers – and prove to himself – how unrelenting Fate can be. At the same time he needs to be more magnanimous and understanding than the people he writes about.

Conrad's people have a profound and haunting quality because they were created by a man who was himself a victim of Fate. He chose between living and writing, as Fate willed him to do, the price demanded for the privilege of becoming an artist. That the life which Fate forced him into accepting would have to be paid for was indicated by those signs of turmoil lurking behind the infant's features. The author is doomed from birth, and it is no surprise that the gallery of people who fought to get out of Conrad's agonised mind are similarly doomed in their different ways. Every novel is born out of a broken heart.

After the tribulations of early life, and having accepted that there is nothing to do but write, the artist is empty of any explicable personality, and passes the rest of his existence trying to find out who he is, creating one person after another in the hope that one of them will be himself. It is part of the unspoken treaty that such a discovery can never be made, though the search goes on for as long as he continues to write.

Conrad had so many conflicting personalities within him trying to get out, each with the potential for tragedy, that he went towards an occupation, and then a culture, which provided the framework enabling him to live within it. The greater the effort, the more successful he would be. A radical change of language provided the most rigid framework of all.

Following the compass of the heart Conrad relinquished the carapace of a ship's captain to take on the protective anonymity of an English country gentleman, so that he would be able to write his novels and stories. Of all his works, *The End of the Tether*, his most pessimistic story, sums up his inner struggle to stay on course having all his life fought the good fight to become the master of his soul, and showed that from being the master of a ship he had become a master of the English novel.

In *The End of the Tether* Captain Whalley, who is going blind, keeps the fact secret because he needs the salary to provide for his daughter, and because he has to recoup the money put into a partnership with the vessel's owner. He must also, according to his social code, maintain his honour until he can voluntarily give up his command. In the event he is forced to succumb to the corruption that all his life he has scorned. By concealing his blindness he is responsible for wrecking the *Sofola*, in that reef-infested region between Pangu and Batu Beru, reefs as lengthily and frighteningly described by Conrad as if he had to go through them himself every day – and that recalled for me those reefs I'd had to be wary of on the pinnace in the Straits of Malacca.

Conrad was fluent in at least five languages, but he chose English to write in, giving rise to the notion that one of the greatest English writers was a Pole. Perhaps he saw the taking on of another language as the final corruption, though one without which he could neither live nor write. Nor could the conventional trappings of an Englishman altogether calm the spiritually violent sea within. The reef-infested region would not allow him to rest easy, all the time fearful that his moral rectitude would be inadvertently deflected by a magnetic lodestone placed malignly near the compass.

His life was spent on a ship that never reached port, having set out from one under the guidance of a chart that allowed for no return. He carried the burden of artist and foreigner, and wrote about people who did not know themselves in an attempt to harness that powerful force which would allow him to know himself and at the same time keep his confidence as an artist. He had all the qualifications for doing this, and those which he did not inherit he forged with the labour of a blacksmith who knows that at any moment his strength might fail.

Introduction to
Great Expectations

Sometime before the Second World War an uncle of mine did a pastel drawing of Bransby Williams, who was playing the role of Magwitch in *Great Expectations*. An amateur artist, he called at the Theatre Royal in Nottingham and cajoled the actor to sit for him during one of the intervals. The features in the drawing that I have before me catch the convict's pathetic human concern for his survival, as well as the savagery with which he assails the 'boy child' Pip, who is wandering around the churchyard at dusk.

Threatened with death by Magwitch (who has escaped from a prison hulk on the nearby Thames), Pip is coerced into stealing food and drink that the runaway desperately needs. The encounter harrows Pip's childhood, and influences the rest of his life.

Charles Dickens, who began writing *Great Expectations* for his magazine *All the Year Round* in December 1860, remembered that *David Copperfield*, published eleven years before, also narrated a boy's childhood in the first person singular. He therefore re-read it, so as to assure his friend and biographer Forster that he had 'fallen into no unconscious repetitions'. He also confessed that he was affected by *David Copperfield* 'to a degree you would hardly believe'.

Most of *Great Expectations* was written at Gad's Hill in Kent: 'so many hours every day for so many days'. Dickens also found time to make a bonfire, in the garden, of his accumulated letters and papers of the previous twenty years, a holocaust that still

147

causes collectors of literary mementos to whiten with shock and disappointment. No doubt such an obliteration of the past gave zest and energy to his work, for the serialisation went on until August of the following year. The novel was universally liked, Carlyle being one of its admirers, though who would not fall under the spell of any work by Charles Dickens?

The awesome encounter of Pip with Magwitch draws us into *Great Expectations*, and the first part of the book is remarkable for the authenticity of the boy's awakening, with its air of hope and cathartic dread.

Pip, an orphan, is being brought up 'by hand', in other words by being beaten and generally knocked about when he is supposed to have misbehaved, by his termagant grown-up sister, known in the locality as Mrs Joe. 'Home,' Pip remarks, with an understatement that prepares him well for the world, 'had never been a very pleasant place to me, because of my sister's temper.' She is married to an illiterate blacksmith, Joe Gargery, who is as kind to young Pip as his wife is unthinking and cruel.

Pip's childhood is plagued by adults who are self-centred and merciless in their attitudes to children. Dickens writes, in 'The Uncommercial Traveller': 'It would be difficult to overstate the intensity and accuracy of an intelligent child's observation. At that impossible time of life, it must sometimes produce a fixed impression. If the fixed impression be an object terrible to the child, it will be (for want of reasoning upon) inseparable from great fear. Force the child at such a time, be Spartan with it, send it into the dark against its will, leave it in a lonely bedroom against its will, and you had better murder it.'

Dickens does far better, by turning Pip into a more human young man than might have been expected after such a childhood, indicating that the characteristics people inherit often enable them to rise above the tormenting circumstances of early life.

Violence is everywhere, not least in the village school: 'The pupils then entered among themselves upon a competitive examination of the subject of boots, with the view of ascertaining who could tread the hardest upon whose shoes.' There seems no place of refuge for Pip, whose harsh sister: 'spoke to me as if she were morally wrenching my teeth out at every reference'. Such physical and mental oppression, which might these days be called abuse, was made tolerable to Pip only by an occasional retreat into fantasy.

As a diversion, which at the same time both saves and damns him – nothing being as simple as it seems in Dickens – Pip receives a summons to meet and entertain the mysterious Miss Havisham. Her rambling dark house is a strange world in which all clocks have been stopped at the same minute.

Pip also meets, and falls in love with, the beautiful child Estella, who undermines the values of his so far unquestioned and humble life. She emphasises her snobbish dislike by dealing out vicious slaps across the face, for no apparent reason. Between Mrs Joe's unremitting persecution, and Miss Havisham's insane pursuit of revenge for her own tragic disappointment, there is little relief.

Estella is Miss Havisham's protégée, and is brought up to take revenge on all young men, being told by her guardian and benefactor: 'Break their hearts, my pride and hope, break their hearts, and have no mercy!'

Estella seems only too willing to practise on young Pip, while she watches Miss Havisham taunt her avaricious relations, who are waiting to get at her money after she dies. They are incensed when she pays for Pip's indentures to train as a blacksmith at the forge of his stepfather. Because of this, Pip later assumes that Miss Havisham is behind the change of fortune that turns him into a 'gentleman'. Embarrassed by his previous life at the blacksmith's house, he yet realises that: 'It is a most miserable thing to feel ashamed of home.'

Wearing fine new clothes on his arrival at Mr Jagger's office in London, he sees a crowd of suppliants for that man's legal services. Two of them, more persistent and excitable than the rest, kiss the hem of Jagger's coat and speak with lisping accents. Pip recognises them as Jews, though the reader might wonder how he could know this when he had not yet been out of his locality to meet anyone who was Jewish.

During his youth Pip sees little difference between certain moral issues, having told no one about helping Magwitch, and made up fantasies to his sister after the first visit to Miss Havisham's. 'Was I not wavering between right and wrong,' he muses, 'when the thing is already done? Such distinctions were no simple matter, though he found the confusion useful when altering his outward identity.

To hint any more at the plot, which has many surprises and is totally engrossing, would spoil the novel for the reader. Dickens requires little intellectual travail, though it has often been said that the people he creates are mere cardboard cutouts and have no depth – a reflection surely on the critic rather than the reader. What he does is expose our hearts to the perils and tribulations of characters we did not previously know, and draws from us emotions we hardly recognise.

Great Expectations is a novel about broken hearts, few of which are mended. Dickens' own heart had been in danger of breaking during his own late childhood, when at the age of twelve he was put to work in a blacking factory, after his father had been taken to prison for debt. The misery of this period marked him for the rest of his life, and though no one can know why anyone becomes a novelist, perhaps Dickens, by writing novel after novel, was able to control the subterranean storm within, at the same time changing the economic conditions of life from those of his childhood.

I have sometimes thought of the novel as not being quite finished when it leaves the author, comparing it in some way to a filmscript. Instead of the novel going to a director who would transfer it to the screen, it reaches the reader who, from the first page, is enabled by the facility of the writing to make a film according to his experience, knowledge, intelligence, imagination and capacity for enjoyment, thus completing the work of the novelist in a more satisfying way than was ever done on a cinema screen, since nothing is left out that the novelist has put in.

The 'development' of the novel has often been discussed as if the art of narrative must continually alter its shape and complexity so as to make it more interesting, even modern, but

Dickens, with the exuberant genius of a poet, had no need of such techniques. The novel does not have to change or die, like any commercial product, as long as it satisfies the need for stories with as wide a range as can be devised by the ingenuity of the novelist. Dickens was first a reader, and he always retained the desire of doing for *his* readers something far better than what had been done for him. One reads for pleasure, and all great novels are a pleasure to read.

Not long after beginning to write I came across that mostly sensible book *Victorian Novelists* by David Cecil, in which from the standpoint of the 1930s he deplored the fact that Dickens, among others, was going out of fashion. His works, usually in collected editions behind glass-fronted bookcases, are, he writes, 'stiff with disuse', but if he were alive today he might notice that Dickens' novels are no longer mentioned 'with boredom, contempt and disgust'. The great writer has 'stood the test of time'.

If the purpose of the novel is to amuse, to inform and to create fear and pity, this does not mean that the story must be imitative or simplistic. Dickens never loses or irritates the reader. The people in *Great Expectations* exist vividly in the mind's eye, as well as in depth. Instead of tedious psychological detail, which can bore when it does not confuse, Dickens, with often exaggerated delineation of speech, as well as of dress and appearance, suggests all the depth to be found within, often leaving us with the illusion that we know his people better than we know ourselves.

As a boy, on my way home from school, I would watch an enormous square hole being dug far below the surface of a building site. Fresh-smelling planks surrounded it, but there was always a chink to spy through. The picture was intensely interesting. Men were working deep down in the excavation, invisible to me, shovelling earth onto a platform above their heads. On that platform, faintly glimpsed, other men spaded it to another platform higher up, and so the process went on until tons of earth reached the surface, to be taken away by lorries.

I have always looked on that operation as an illustration of how the novelist must work in getting at the secrets of the human heart. He also digs and delves, and through language, intuition, the labour of writing, and going as far down as his imagination can penetrate, shapes a story out of what he has discovered.

Novelists are often united by an accurate sense of the landscape in their work. Conrad, Hardy and D H Lawrence come to mind. In *Great Expectations* Dickens described the Cooling Marshes at all seasons, recreating a world hard to forget. In the summer of 1982 I set out on the twenty-mile walk from Gravesend to Rochester, the first part of a hike along the Saxon Shore Way to Rye in Kent.

The route led, on a hot, dry day, along the southern side of the Thames Estuary and then inland to Cooling, whose featureless marshes had little to remind me of the scenes in *Great Expectations*. Instead of convict hulks on the river the huge white superstructure of a container ship glided by. Yet sitting in Cooling churchyard to eat bread and cheese, before going for a pint of shandy to the pub where Joe Gargery spent many an hour away from his fierce wife, something of the sombre atmosphere and loneliness of the place came back.

Needless to say, I had a small bound copy of the novel in my rucksack, and there were many points along the route where it was impossible to resist reading a page or so while resting my sore feet. At the same time I had to ration myself if the book was to last the whole trip, and enable me to devour a chapter or two at each bed and breakfast place before going upstairs to sleep. *Great Expectations* is that kind of book.

D H Lawrence and District

'I have no allocated place in the world of things, I do not belong to Beldover [Eastwood] nor to Nottingham nor to England nor to this world, but they none of them exist, I am trammelled and entangled in them, but they are unreal. I must break out of it, like a nut from its shell, which is an unreality.'

This equally applied to D H Lawrence (1885–1930) but he gave the words instead – being a novelist – to his recalcitrant heroine Ursula Brangwen at the end of *The Rainbow*, published in 1915. If one may relate these sentiments to him, and square them with his actions, then he did indeed break out of Eastwood and district where he was born and brought up, going far beyond that 'dry, brittle corruption spreading over the face of the land'.

His mother died of cancer in 1910:

> 'The sun was immense and rosy
> Must have sunk and become extinct
> The night you closed your eyes forever against me.'

As if she had decided to die so that he could make his way alone in the world.

The road was clear. He jettisoned the sweetheart of his youth, Jessie Chambers (Miriam Leivers in the novels), a painful, if not agonising process, and absconded with Frieda von Richthofen, wife of Professor Weekley. Eastwood was finished, rubbed away like the chalked ciphers from a teacher's blackboard, as he no

153

doubt thought. Like many English provincial writers, he 'did not like it here'.

His impulse was to get away, to strike out with the only means readily to hand, a woman. And the woman he chose, or who was chosen for him or, indeed, chose him, took up with another man as the only possibility to get out of a deadly and failed marriage. Lawrence took his first love, his mother, from his father, and his last love from her husband. And if it was these two women who chose him this might suggest that he was the sort of man who could do little without being chosen. The second vital choosing was a logical continuation of the first.

Why did he fall in love with Frieda? The fact that she was German, with family in another land, had much to do with it. She was a few years older, already married, a mother of three children, so knew what she wanted. She was exotic and flamboyant and unknown, but he had hopes of getting to know her, though at that stage, carried along without such questions, by a blind whim of fate, it has no importance. Even so, he must have had doubts about what he was doing, doubts he puts into the mind of Jimmy in his story 'Jimmy and the Desperate Woman', who is in a similar situation. The world is full of young men who, on the surface at least, do not know what they want until meeting someone who realises so well what they want that they act on it with little hesitation. It rarely takes two to act.

Eastwood was dead, so long live the world. In the mountains of Bavaria, Nottinghamshire fell into its dark and to him deserved oblivion. Long live the sun, and welcome to distant vistas. Whom did he leave behind? A father he had been brought up to detest, and whom he would have disliked in any case. The father was a living example of what Lawrence might easily have become, because much of the father existed in him, under the writer's clever and protecting skin – the less robust version of his father, who easily took to violence in his quarrels with Frieda.

Lawrence left brothers and sisters and friends behind. When he went back from time to time he saw a dying landscape as far as his spiritual needs were concerned, for it lost its attraction after his mother died, an event that laid waste his youth. One has to live youth to the full so as to get rid of it effectively, and from then on youth and Eastwood came to life only in his novels. He learned to keep the area in its place, but buried deeply enough so that it no longer tormented. The more he wrote, the more its reality died. Not only did he leave it, but the theme of departure occurred in many of his novels, as with Alvina Houghton at the end of *The Lost Girl*, and Aaron Sisson in *Aaron's Rod*. At the end of *The White Peacock* the bankrupt farmer is considering a new life in Canada, and Paul Morel could not tolerate the place any longer after the last six lines of *Sons and Lovers*, while Gerald in *Women in Love* found his snowy womb in the solitude of the Alps.

The fact of not liking it there, once he had left it, mattered very much to Lawrence. The intelligent and hypersensitive shell that he had to live within accepted the landscapes of other countries, and if he came back now and again to Eastwood it was not even as a tourist, but like a health visitor wondering whether to call in the corporation stoving gangs, either to disinfect or destroy the place.

The longer he was away from Nottinghamshire the more he hated what he saw as its ugliness, an emphasis that increased the longer his absences, as if to defend himself against the charge of having so heartlessly left it, and given up certain people who had done so much for him. In his own estimation Jessie Chambers was one of these, and in view of his difficulties with the amoral Frieda, how often must he have regretted that he had ever left.

Plain enough at the end of *The Rainbow*, his obsession with the landscape's ugliness increased, the theme going through most of his novels and stories in which 'The North' appears, until the final ranting of Mellors the gamekeeper, in *Lady Chatterley's Lover*, in which young colliers are scorned for going to dances in Mansfield on their motorbikes, as if they didn't deserve such good fortune, or would be better off knitting blankets under the greenwood tree.

Lawrence was drawn to strong men, though hated his father, unable to realise the reasons for his sometimes brutish behaviour. Women had the most influence on his fateful decisions, which is not unusual. He was dominated by his mother, guided by Jessie

Chambers, and driven (at times half mad) by Frieda, suggesting that a man of his sensibility and passionate talent can have few meaningful women in his life.

Another factor in his work and life was love of landscape. On his travels he was taken – you could say infatuated – by grandiose and dangerous scenery, features of the earth that were strong because they were asleep. But maybe the truest love of his life continued to be that significant magic circle of which Eastwood was the centre. 'That's the country of my heart,' he said, echoing Richard Jeffries, in a long letter to Ralph Gardner, from Florence at the end of 1926. In various novels and stories the Eastwood locality had many made-up labels: Beldover, Netherthorpe, Woodhouse or Teversall. He loved the beauties of the area till he died, with that intensity that comes with absence, but what he considered to be the ugliness of the area he increasingly fulminated against.

The region responsible for his rage and choler was in fact neither totally ugly nor completely beautiful, but a jumble of ambiguities that found a reflection in himself. The scars and wounds of still working industrialism on the Nottinghamshire–Derbyshire border gave Lawrence the emotive force of his descriptive genius, provided the creative energy of his pen, which he early recognised, and acted as a catalyst for him to write such lyrical prose about those half-concealed areas that were so beautiful they highlighted the ugliness around. This ambivalent attitude comes out of his poem *The North Country*:

> 'The air is dark with north and sulphur, the
> grass is a darker green
> And the people darkly invested with purple move
> Palpably through the scene.'

The landscape was ugly, but existence in those days meant a constant fight against grime and dirt to keep house and family clean. Soot from factory and workshop chimneys, smoke from coal fires in every house, dung on the streets from horse transport, men coming black and neanderthal home from the pits and washing at the kitchen sink or in a tin bath before the fire. Some women did better than others, in that a scrubbed doorstep was often an indication of the standard of cleanliness within. There were outside earth closets (you could get wet 'walking across the yard') and not the flushing inside toilets of today; and continually smoking coal fires which, at the end of the day, had to be scraped free of ash and clinker for the morning, which process, if not done carefully, sent dust all over the room. Cooking also had to be done on coal or wood stoves. No one complained, because that was all there was at such a time.

It was not so much the domestic squalor that Lawrence raged against. My grandmother kept a sweet-smelling clean kitchen and house, the only illumination being from oil lamps, coal and wood for cooking and heating, an outside lavatory, and all water brought in buckets from a well some distance away.

Much of Lawrence's hatred for urban and industrial landscape was influenced by the three women in his early life, views that found ready agreement in himself, an attitude that never left him. It would have obsessed anyone with a sensitive eye towards landscape. He also inherited the prejudices of English writers, who bewailed the ruination of rural England, towns and cities being regarded as hell, and villages a more natural way of existence. One ought to read such real-life accounts as *Lark Rise to Candleford* for a proper perspective on the matter, as far as rural living was concerned. The former attitudes die hard, however, with its longing for peace and non-involvement.

Lawrence was isolationist in that he saw little but deadliness in the spread of nineteenth-century industrialism, such extreme views leading him to despise people more than was good either for him or his writing. His early novels, up to *The Rainbow*, are the best because he is tender and just to his characters, but after that the humanity seems to go out of his portrayals.

He also had to get away from England because of the suffocating class atmosphere of Edwardian and Georgian days. In Italy or Germany or Mexico an Englishman was more likely to be accepted as a 'gentleman' no matter how poor he appeared to be. If his aristocratic wife washed the sheets in their Italian cottage – though more often Lawrence did it himself – it was merely a mark of eccentricity.

In his youth he said to Jessie Chambers that people would think it silly for a coalminer's son to write poetry, and he could not imagine himself becoming a writer of any sort among people of such limited attitudes. He was unable to expose himself to those who couldn't understand him, finding it a situation impossible to fight against and so, sooner or later, he had to get as far away from them as he could.

Before the age of thirty Lawrence had all the promise of becoming a great writer, while after it he became something of a crank in the views he expounded, which did not have a good effect on his work, apart from the first half of *The Lost Girl*, most of which was written before he was thirty. Many shorter novels were good, as well as some stories and poems and also (though not published till 1920) the part of *Kangaroo* in which he excoriated the treatment he received from the British nation he was almost called up to defend during the First World War. Much of the later work is tendentious, some of it hardly possible to read. Prophet and philosopher were roles he assumed on being influenced by people he met after starting out on his travels, though it's possible he needed little pushing.

The 1920s was not a good period for English writing, if I think of the works of J Cowper Powys, Henry Williamson and Wyndham Lewis, all of whom seemed to write more from the head than the heart.

Lawrence looked back on Eastwood to create his own lyrical backwater of idealised scenery. He wandered around the world for the rest of his life, though if there had been no Reformation in England he might have spent more time at Eastwood. Instead he went to those Catholic parts of the world dominated by the female spirit of the Virgin Mary, and the mother-worship of the Latins. Either that or, as in Mexico, he superimposed his talent onto Aztec notions of the sun, resulting in a very strange mixture indeed.

After *The Lost Girl* (1920) and *Women in Love* (1921) he began to lose the reality of local topography. In *Lady Chatterley's Lover* it seemed as if he were writing about the sort of black dream country neither human nor real. But though he left his beloved acres behind, he had, for better or worse, gained contact with other areas of his soul through travelling. No matter what his final motives (and whoever knows what they were?), he gained the world, while the most generous part of his spirit remained in Nottinghamshire.

He was, in fact, born only a mile away from Derbyshire. You walk down the hill of the main road out of Eastwood until coming to the railway station on the right – now smashed and boarded up – then cross the canal and the meagre Erewash, and you are out of Byron's county. After another dozen miles you are in the Pennines at Matlock. The ugliness has gone. Picturesque though sometimes claustrophobic valleys and wide open hill ranges are all around, with enough scenic beauty to satisfy anyone, only a few hours' bike ride from Nottingham and even less from Eastwood.

After I was fourteen and went to work, and had saved up enough to buy a bicycle, I took that road to Matlock, sometimes alone, occasionally with friends, puffing up and out of Nottingham through Aspley and Cinderhill. A colliery at the latter place was called Tinder Hill in *Sons and Lovers*, and in Lawrence's time a bumpy stretch of road ran over it, over which the father of Paul Morel, injured in the mine, was taken on a cart to Nottingham Hospital, the subject of his moving dialect poem, '*The Collier's Wife*'.

Beyond Eastwood a free-wheeling down to the Erewash was followed by a sure push up to Codnor and Ripley, then down again to the Derwent and along the winding valley to Matlock. At that time, knowing nothing of D H Lawrence (I didn't begin to read his books till I was 21), I went one Easter weekend beyond Matlock, through Bakewell and Buxton to Chapel-en-le-Frith, spending a couple of nights in barns by the roadside, then back to Nottingham via Chesterfield and Clay Cross. The hills were beautiful to look at, and I in no way hated the hilltop mining towns when back among them. Coming from the built-up protection of Nottingham, I felt comforted by the frequent appearance of such places. At Easter the road was often wet, and the wind bitter enough, but the impulse was to wear out the body after a week in the factory, and get as far from the city as one could in a long weekend.

On a single day's run I cycled the 25 miles to Matlock, climbed the Heights of Abraham of several hundred feet, visited the ancient lead-workings of the Rutland Cavern, rowed on the slate-grey Derwent for an hour and got as near to the weir as I could without going over or having to be rescued by an irate boatman, then beat the darkness back to Nottingham, all on a bottle of milk or lemonade and a packet of sandwiches.

The first novel I read by Lawrence was *The Rainbow*. Up to then nothing had been as familiar, nor as electrifying:

> The Brangwens had lived on the Marsh Farm, in the meadows where the Erewash twisted sluggishly through alder trees, separating Derbyshire from Nottinghamshire. Two miles away, a church-tower stood on a hill, the house of the little country town climbing assiduously up to it. Whenever one of the Brangwens in the fields lifted his head from his work, he saw the church-tower of Ilkeston in the empty sky.

I knew exactly what he was writing about, from walking across those fields, and seeing the same view. Later in the novel Tom Brangwen goes beyond the Erewash, on horseback to Matlock, and encounters the foreigner in the hotel whom he 'loved . . . for his exquisite graciousness, for his tact and reserve, and for his ageless, monkey-like self-surety'.

Lawrence made ambivalent comments about foreigners in his books and letters all his life, as if by marrying one he had the right to do so, though mixing his parochial views with those of Edwardian upper-class people he met after leaving Eastwood made such prejudices hardly noticeable.

Brangwen's encounter with the foreigner at Matlock created a change of horizon that led him to propose to Anna Lensky, the widow of a Polish exile, who had come to work as a housekeeper at Cossethay (Cossall) vicarage.

Tom Brangwen, the grandfather of Ursula, lived at the nearby Marsh, where before the Reformation there had been a Benedictine cell or chapel of St Thomas – according to Britton's topographical work on Nottinghamshire (based on Thoroton's *Antiquities*) – which Lawrence obviously knew about, and so gave the saint's name to his main character.

Cossall and the Marsh is now divided from Nottingham by the M1 motorway, a whole wood uprooted to make room for a service area. Tom Brangwen died on driving home one wet and stormy night after a drinking bout at the Angel in Nottingham, a notorious pub that had, in fact, been pulled down half a century earlier. Blind drunk and half asleep, Brangwen was drawn along by his horse in the dark and muddy lane, through Bilborough and Strelley, and when close to home he drowned in the floodwaters swirling around his farm, the Erewash canal nearby having burst its banks while he had been away.

Concerning the numerous places in which an author makes his characters attempt to sort out their destinies, and imagining they were acting them through, it is interesting to connect each one with the real name, using the few lines of description allotted to each.

Lawrence sometimes uses actual names, but often made-up ones, and whether an event is of vital importance or not, it is pure chance or whim which one it might be. Many such places can be traced. A stream called the Dumbles forms Nethermere Valley, steep and wooded hills along its course to the North and South, but covering a smaller area than Lawrence's description implies – as was often the case with Thomas Hardy's Wessex landscapes. The cleft of Nethermere was lush and wet in late spring when I went there recently, approaching from Annesley. Almost hidden from the road is Strelley Mill, the Felley Mill Farm of *The White Peacock*.

Such topographical identifications are uncertain: after much tramping and detective work one might say: 'I am sitting on the same fence Ursula Brangwen got over in fear and panic when the horses chased her, at the end of *The Rainbow*', but it may not have been the place at all. Nor would it matter if it were. Lawrence sometimes made it easy to find out, but we will never finally know. Yet the mental maps of his native ground were fairly accurate, as one sees on spreading a one-inch sheet, to find that in his novels he tended to rename places the closer they were to Eastwood, while further away it did not matter, and he gave real names.

Eastwood was not a cut-off mining village, but a well-known place in Nottinghamshire. There were hikers, cyclists, trams and people out on 'mystery trips', who might not know where they were because they'd already stopped at too many pubs to care, though usually they knew only too well, for each bus had its traveller who had been to every place in the county, and perhaps out of it as well, as a soldier or sailor. Eastwood was a half-way house through which thousands of people passed to reach Matlock and the Pennines.

There were wealthy houses and rich people in the area. People flocked through the main street of Eastwood to the spas and pleasure haunts of the Peak District, but in most directions outside the place it is half town and half country, slum and mansion, headstock and folly, redbrick and priory ruins, lime kiln and green glen, farm houses and ironworks, such a mixture making the landscape vast in small mileages, an exploring ground that baffles yet eventually opens the mind.

In the nineteenth century Lord Palmerston contributed to the founding of the Mechanics Institute at Eastwood. Coal had been mined in the neighbourhood for centuries, and regular wages, however small, gave it a certain glow of liveliness and prosperity. In 1812 Britton, paraphrasing Thoroton no doubt, wrote that, 'those who chuse to gossip with the sage chroniclers of the place, will be told a wonderful story of a farmer being swallowed up alive in the parlour of the village alehouse, while he was swallowing a cup of ale, to the great surprise of the host, who by this means discovered that his humble mansion was built on an exhausted coal pit.'

Close to the Erewash Valley, Eastwood had access by canal to the Trent, which gave an opening to the Humber beyond Gainsborough, and hence to the coast. The main line from London to Manchester ran up the Erewash Valley, with trains stopping at Pye Bridge a few miles away. In *Sons and Lovers* the station is called Sethley Bridge, and Paul Morel goes with his sister (Lawrence himself and Ada) to meet their brother William coming home for Christmas from London.

The train was more than two hours late, and they were anxious about the meat getting overcooked at home, but they waited in the evening frost, such cold being forgotten when following handsome but ill-fated William, carrying his Gladstone bag, into the house.

Paul's mother in the novel takes him one afternoon to visit Mrs Leivers at Willey Farm (Haggs Farm) three miles away, where he meets Miriam the daughter. The account of their long association makes *Sons and Lovers* one of the finest novels of adolescent love in the English language.

At nineteen Paul goes with Miriam and others on an excursion to the Hemlock Stone, a long walk there and back. At the time he worked at Jordan's factory in Nottingham, earning twenty shillings a week. Lawrence was employed for a few months in a similar factory (Heywood's, manufacturers of surgical appliances) at the age of fifteen, but his appropriate counterpart in *Sons and Lovers* stayed some three years.

The happy group crossed the railway line and went into Ilkeston, 'a town of idleness and lounging. At Stanton Gate the iron foundry blazed' (as it did still in my day, during the Second World War). At Trowel they crossed again from Derbyshire into Nottinghamshire. Crowds of other Easter trippers were at the Hemlock Stone, out for the day from the city. Paul 'found the stone disappointing...a little, gnarled, twisted stump of rock, something like a decayed mushroom, standing out pathetically on the side of a field.'

Members of the party began carving their initials, 'but Paul desisted, because he had read in the newspaper satirical remarks about initial carvers, who could find no other road to immortality' as if he knew even then that his route to such an arcane place would be different and more sure. The last time I was there railings had been put around it.

In Britton's book the Hemlock Stone is more flatteringly described, perhaps not so weather-beaten a century earlier: 'Between these hills, on the brow of a rising ground, is a very curious and conspicuous object, called the "Hemlockstone". This is an insulated rugged mass of rock, or reddish sandstone, upwards of thirty feet high, and consisting of very thin *laminae* dipping to the West; its extreme breadth from north to south is about twelve feet at the base, but spreading at about two-thirds of its elevation; and its thickness below is about four feet. In outline, it bears some slight resemblance to a mushroom, and is evidently wearing away, from the effects of the weather.'

The Hemlock Stone was said by some to be a pagan relic, always a favourite picnic point for people from that side of Nottingham. The rock is surmounted by two broad distinct masses of hard-wearing green ragstone, thus given it the mushroom appearance. The name of Hemlock Stone comes from the colour of the plant, but by some misdirection of primitive logic it was said that to run seven times around the stone was a sure cure for rheumatism, though anyone with such a complaint would hardly be able to make a single circuit.

On their return to Eastwood Miriam goes back along the lane to look for Paul, to find that he's lagged behind to mend his mother's umbrella. The effect of the Hemlock Stone on them was said to have been insignificant, but Miriam 'always regarded that sudden coming upon him in the lane as a revelation'. It was the first sign of their relationship deepening into a love that both were afraid of, but sensed might last forever because they would not know how to end it.

The Hemlock Stone was a fair way from the city in those days, but now it is no longer so isolated, with new houses on Stapleford Hill immediately behind. I often walked along the canal, or cycled there from the Balloon Houses. The lane where

Miriam came upon Paul Morel absorbed in mending his mother's umbrella 'as a revelation' might have been that part where it bridges the motorway.

Paul and Miriam also go to Wingfield Manor. They take a train to Alfreton, and visit the church: 'The place was decorated for Easter. In the front hundreds of white narcissi seemed to be growing. The air was dim and coloured from the windows and thrilled with a subtle scent of lilies and narcissi. In that atmosphere Miriam's soul came to a glow. Paul was afraid of the things he mustn't do and he was sensitive to the feel of the place. Miriam turned to him. He answered. They were together.'

'It was past midday when they climbed the steep path to Wingfield Manor', one of the finest ruins in Britain. Lawrence had the steady absorbent eye of young genius in these early novels, never to be surpassed in later work. He had youth and love on his side and, just as important, a land he considered his own.

It mattered more than he knew at the time. Place is everything, odorous soil at the feet, the nostrils clouded with soot and pollen, the first smells and sounds of life, cold grass bending under frost in winter, scorched bracken in the summer. Youth is so strong that hope doesn't yet weigh in the scales. Life simply is. Everything is in unison, tragic fate unknowingly burning away, or youth coolly observing it while not caring to do much about it. Lawrence was early on determined to break up that unity, and knew that leaving the place would propel him towards an intensity that would die on him if he dallied and stayed where he was.

If Lawrence hadn't been born in Nottinghamshire he would have been a different writer. England is full of small countries. Like all other nations, perhaps, for better or worse, dozens of little class, race and geographical divisions that defy analysis or sociological investigation, and only writers are capable of charting a way through them to tackle the fundamental issues beneath. I don't suppose Stendhal would have been the same writer if he hadn't been born in Grenoble, nor Balzac at Tours. But while place is everything, we are born as ships at sea as far as our souls are concerned, no matter how solid the earth on which we walk.

I know Eastwood and the surrounding countryside, having covered every lane and footpath from an early age on forays out of Nottingham, either on foot or by that greatest invention of modern times, the bicycle. A favourite place was Misk Hill, the nearest point to the city over five hundred feet high, from which I could look down over the whole area. Hucknall Torkard church is nearby, where Byron's tomb is kept, and Lawrence's father used to sing in Newstead Abbey choir as a boy.

From the summit one can also see the church at Eastwood three miles away, the same spire Paul and Miriam gazed at from Crich Hill in the other direction. On their way to Wingfield Manor, such surveys of triangulation fix themselves in the heart and stay there.

At thirteen Lawrence won a scholarship to Nottingham High School, whose buildings had a forbidding and exclusive aspect when I passed them as a child. Though not far from where I lived, it was a different sort of district, and a group of us, to show our disapproval of the place, would throw sour apples over the wall, on the way back from plundering orchards on the outskirts of the town.

Lawrence's mother had been a teacher, and he was brought up to have no such antipathy. An intelligent child, he liked the school, and went on to become a teacher at Ilkeston, and at 21 to do botany at Nottingham University College. The modern-day university is at High Fields near to Beeston, and Lawrence satirised it in his poem. I don't suppose he would have approved of my having received an honorary degree there in 1988:

> In Nottingham, that dismal town
> where I went to school and college,
> they've built a new university
> for a new dispensation of knowledge.

The boating lake and swimming pool in the grounds of the university made it a place to enjoy, after the crowded streets of Radford. Coming the other way, from London or Derby, the university is the first sign of Nottingham seen from the train.

The long grey building, on rising ground, beyond an evenly spaced line of poplars like a row of candles, has a square tower set in the middle, the whole like a slab of iced cake ready to be enjoyed.

Every time I see it from the train window it is hard not to notice what a wonderful field of fire there is from its southerly windows, commanding the Trent Valley and two main roads into the city. The boating lake could act as an outer defence work, skilfully narrowing the approaches and canalising routes of attack, so that any assailants would have little chance of reaching the main buildings.

A mile or so east from the university is Nottingham Castle, ugly and menacing enough until one goes into the art gallery and sees the paintings of Dame Laura Knight, or stands on the southern terrace to look over the Meadows district, no longer a mass of streets and small factories, but studded with council flats – much cleaner, though it's a puzzle to get into the area by car.

There are no more colliery headstocks around the town of Eastwood either. A bypass makes the place harder to find but, once in the main street of Hilltop, I doubt that Lawrence would disapprove of the lack of smells and grit, though he might cock an eye at the small museum installed into his birthplace under the auspices of Enid Goodband.

Cyril, the hero of *The White Peacock*, went to the Castle with Meg. 'We stood on the high rock in the cool of the day and watched the sun sloping over the great river-flats where the menial town spread out, and ended, while the river and meadows continued in the distance.' When the young Paul Morel wins first prize in a painting competition his picture is exhibited in the museum with others. Lawrence began drawing and painting at an early age, though there is no evidence that he won any competition. The proprietor of the hotel at Taos in New Mexico, where Lawrence lived for a time, has a collection of paintings by him on the walls of a back room, and charges a dollar a time to whoever wants to see them.

From Nottingham Castle the wooded escarpment of Clifton beyond the Trent is visible, with the Grove running along the top, where Henry Kirk White walked and wrote his melancholy verses, before dying of consumption at 21. The wide two-mile grove of elm, beech and oak trees goes along a level ridge, and Paul Morel in *Sons and Lovers* walked there with Clara after breaking with Miriam. He and Clara scrambled down through the foliage to the swiftly flowing river, the bank so steep that, if not for the bushes, it would send one straight into the water.

Paul and Clara go on to Clifton village, and 'the old lady at whose house they had tea was roused into gaiety by them.' I remember the cottage also as a favourite place to have tea with your girl after a country walk and some courting up the Grove. Now there's a housing estate nearby, and the buildings of Trent University, so maybe the cottage no longer exists.

Those whom the gods love die young, but those whom the gods despise are in danger of staying young. Lawrence was determined to leave Nottingham and his youth, so that the gods would have no cause to pursue him. The place meant too much for him to put up with it any longer. He had suffered a great deal, and had learned enough to know that there was nothing else but to leave. His mother had died, and he had broken with Jessie Chambers due to what he considered her too intense and possessive love. He was, she said, a man who had to have all decisions made for him, and she had connived in this for a long time, until sensing that maybe he wasn't her kind of man after all, because he had accepted the notion too readily, and she thought there should be more to a man than that. In any case there were, finally, some decisions over which she could have no control. The truth was that he wanted a woman who would have more control over him than Jessie ever could, something she would not submit to.

After Nottingham University College Lawrence worked as a teacher in London, though still not free of his youth. There was little to hold him to such a state, but how was he to get away from it? It was as if he had devoured life before it could consume him entirely – a contest of self-annihilation before breath itself ran out. He needed the great and final change in order to survive, the vital break that would enable him to go on as an artist.

There was little to keep him in Eastwood. He had already published *The White Peacock*, had written *The Trespasser* and was working on *Sons and Lovers*. Though he could write those early novels while connected to home ground, he could not do so with the autobiographical *Sons and Lovers*. To translate pain and love into art he needed to be at a distance, and *Sons and Lovers* was finished in Italy, when birthplace and youth were behind him.

All that had nurtured and tormented him had to be put beyond the horizon, in every possible way. He met Frieda and eloped to Germany, a love affair that led to her divorce, and marriage to Lawrence in 1915.

They stayed together till his death in the south of France in 1930, when he was 44. There were signs in his writing at the time that he was ready for the second great leap of his creative life. The emergence from youth in his twenties had lifted him from a phase that his spirit found insupportable. Now, that phase long spent, it was time to move on. But life is not a series of little boxes, and he was critically ill from tuberculosis. The cost of making the first great break robbed him of the primal life force necessary to carry him to the greatest accomplishments of his writing life.

He had travelled over much of the world in eighteen years, but though Nottinghamshire was still used for many of his novels and stories, the bucolic intensity of his first books was lacking, and what took its place did nothing to satisfy his embittered heart.

The last-of-England paragraphs from *The Lost Girl* were a reflection of his feelings on departing from England after the Great War, during which he had been persecuted for having a German wife: 'For there, behind all the sunshine, was England, England beyond the water, rising with ash-grey corpse-grey cliffs, and streaks of snow on the downs above. England, like a long ash-grey coffin, slowly submerging.'

Robert Tressell

*T*he *Ragged Trousered Philanthropists* is a novel about a group
of house painters and decorators, and their families, in
Muggsborough (Hastings) around the year 1906. It describes the
workman's life of that time, the subjection, deception and in
many cases destitution of people whose labour created the luxury
and glitter of the Edwardian Age, a time that those who did not
have to live in it often imagine to have been 'the good old days'
of pomp and circumstance, the apex of England's greatness, the
time before 1914, when everyone was supposed to know his
place and because of it was contented and grateful. Those who
had money not only lived off the fat of the land but off the lean
of the people as well.

While reading the abridged Penguin version of Tressell's book
– I was serving with the air force in Malaya – it became obvious
that the writer, in not calling it '*The Ragged Arsed Philanthropists*'
had chosen the more proper-sounding title knowing that
otherwise it wouldn't be published. It almost never was. The book
was lent to me by a fellow wireless operator from Liverpool, who
said: 'You should read this. Among other things it's the book that
won the '45 Election for Labour.'

Cut to half length, it seemed strangely put together, ending on
a note of despair, suggesting that cranks who believed in socialism
and the impossibility of it ever coming about could do nothing
better than think of suicide. Paperback editions published in the

1960s end the way the author intended, and give a somewhat different impression.

It's hard to say what effect the book had on me at first reading, but it has haunted me ever since. Those who know something about the misery depicted by Robert Tressell can get much out of it: a bolstering of class feeling, pure rage, or a call to action, maybe a beneficial dose of all three, but the novel finally transcends a call to class warfare in its evocation of pure tragedy, and description of the human jungle among the lowly employed. The pity is that the writer didn't live to give us more of his work.

Owen, the main character, tries with patience and ingenuity to enlighten his workmates as to how social justice could level out the wealth and give them not only a little more to live on, but also hope of alleviating their inequalities for good. They either won't listen, or mock him for his trouble, so he dubs them 'philanthropists', benefactors in tattered trousers, who willingly hand over the results of their labour to employers and the rich. They think it the natural order of things that the rich should exploit them, that 'gentlemen' are the only people with the right to govern, a worthwhile theme, though Tressell's personal and often amusing detail keeps the book a novel and not a tract.

The workmen seem to feel that the cruel and hierarchical scheme within which they exist offers no possibility of advancement, realising that in such a lowly state success can only be achieved on the backs of their mates. Ambition can only exist as a dream, heavenly bread to sustain them in their suffering while deprived of all but the barest amount of earthly bread.

A higher form of dignity awaits them if only they will act, though Owen can't finally tell them how to do so, afraid as they are of the social void that would come about if they did rise up. Such a stalemate gives the book its fiery energy, because in reality there is no way out.

Robert Tressell (born Robert Noonan) was himself a workman, so knew what he was talking about. In 1911 he left his wife in Hastings and went to Liverpool, intending to work on the docks until he had saved enough money to emigrate to America, and when he earned enough money there he would send for them, but he died of tuberculosis, aged forty, before he could leave, and was buried in a pauper's grave.

By 1914 his daughter was old enough to go into service, at the house of Grant Richards, the London publisher. Hearing talk of books at the table one evening, she mentioned afterwards that her father had written one, and the manuscript was in her trunk upstairs. As a result the novel appeared a few months later, but in a much shortened and cut-about version. Many and varied editions have appeared since then, and sold tens of thousands of copies all over the world.

Strange to say, one of my first thoughts after finishing the book in Malaya was that it hadn't been written by a working man, thereby showing those symptoms of faithlessness that so enraged Owen. This impression may have been because publishers and editors had tampered with the book, though we now have as full a version as possible from the box of manuscript saved by his daughter.

Fifteen years after that first reading I came across *Tressell of Mugsborough* by F C Ball, Tressell's dedicated and indefatigable biographer, and a novelist himself. He quotes the following, written by a relation of Tressell's: 'I have told you quite truthfully that Robert was not born into the working class. He would have had a very much happier life, no doubt, had he been.' Tressell was grafted on to working-class life through family misfortune, though little is known about his early years, except that his father was an inspector in the Royal Irish Constabulary.

In 1974 F C Ball wrote a more definitive biography of Tressell's life, showing how he grieved for the people around him, fulminating against their poverty as well as his own. His Irish descent, with his talent and outstanding passion, justified his detestation of much English callousness and hypocrisy regarding his antecedents. Sick though he was with the disease that was to kill him, he nevertheless had to work, and in his spare time produced the first profound novel of English working-class life. A generation before had appeared Arthur Morrison's *A Child of the Jago* and

Tales of Mean Streets, and though they are still worth reading, he wrote from too far outside his characters, unlike Tressell, who put his people into perspective by relating them to society as a whole.

Many familiar with Tressell's book talk about its characters – such as Crass the chargehand, Misery the foreman, Rushton the firm's director, and Owen the 'socialist' workman, as well as the women and children who suffer the most – as if they knew them, and recount incidents as if they had happened before their eyes only the other day. What makes the book unique is its humour, and utterly unsentimental code of honour. You can laugh at the way tragic things are told, while being led through the fire, only to weep when cold blasts greet you at the other end.

The theme of class warfare in *The Ragged Trousered Philanthropists* elevates it into tragedy. Some may think that working people are not worth writing about because they have few refinements of perception and that lack of intelligence denies them the means of self-expression, and that people who can't express themselves are not good enough material for the novelist – which may be true if the novelist has neither sympathy nor imagination, nor knowledge of their plight. Self-expression denied to participants in Greek drama gave rise to tragedy of mythic proportions. Defoe would have recognised *The Ragged Trousered Philanthropists* as the classic that it is.

The inability to obtain bread and shelter means illness and death, and goes back even beyond the concepts of tragedy or myth. The attempt to get more than bread, as well as self-respect and the dignity of spiritual bread, is a theme that can emulate myth while still containing the seeds of tragic failure, as in Owen's case, and that of Robert Tressell, who sensed a greater significance in the fight to obtain a more equitable share of the good things of life than in wallowing hopelessly in a state already at the end of its spiritual tether.

Tressell's workmen had class feeling to the extent that they regarded themselves as totally inferior. Seeing no way out of their predicament, they could only say, 'It's not for the likes of us', and improvement to their lives was only permissible in ways laid down by their 'betters'. Owen knew that his harangues would solve nothing. The 'not for the likes of us' attitude (not, thank God, so widespread any more) fostered the poisonous sloth of self-pity. The only way out was for them to transcend their stupidity and find the solution in their own hearts. Tragically, he did not see how this could happen, because their hearts had already been taken from them. In exchange for more bread they would have no foresight to demand anything else. The middle class wouldn't, and perhaps couldn't, help them. Only what the workers take is helpful. What they are given is useless.

Owen's workmates needed more help than they were able to accept. Those in the jungle are only powerful when they try to get out of it, but Owen's realisation that they will never do so makes him a tragic figure. Today the novel is simply a good book but, like all journeys through hell, it has its own excitement, harmony, and pathos, while being witty and instructive.

Owen's utter rejection of English middle-class values was no doubt related to his feelings of outrage, after his early days as a more independent workman in South Africa. The working men in England did not have the same knowledge and spirit as we are led to believe they had during the Industrial Revolution. Never before or since had they been so oppressed. The best went to the Dominions, the hopeless stayed behind.

England was stagnating in a materialistic backwater of self-satisfaction and callous indifference, a society in which those who 'had' hoped it would go on forever, and those who 'had not' were beginning to regret the day they were born. As Owen says late in the book: 'All around was a state of dreadful anarchy: abundant riches, luxury, vice, hypocrisy, poverty, starvation, and crime. Men literally fighting with each other for the privilege of working for their bread, and little children crying with hunger and cold and slowly perishing of want.'

By the time this novel about the class war was published, those who might have acted in a revolution – if they had listened to Owen – were being butchered on the Western Front. Owen was made to say, in his prophetic frenzy: 'In every country, myriads of armed men were waiting for their masters to give them the signal to fall upon and rend each other like wild beasts.'

The Great War drained off the surplus blood of unemployment and incipient unrest. It proved once more the maxim that war is the father of a certain kind of progress. A shilling a day, food and clothing, even the possibility of foreign travel, was something the ragged-trousered philanthropists hadn't had before. They welcomed it, for a while, then died 'tearing the guts out of the German army' on the Somme and at Paschendaele. Such ferocious patriotism as was shown, as well as courage, endurance and ferocity, was that which Owen would have liked them to display in a revolution. It would, however, have surprised him if they had.

Arnold Bennett: The Man from the North

When *The Old Wives' Tale* was published in the autumn of 1908, Arnold Bennett said to his wife: 'This is the most important day of my life! I've done my best. I shall never be able to do anything better.' It is a familiar utterance from a novelist, and no doubt Bennett made it once or twice more, though in this case he happened to be right. If *he* didn't know, who could? None of his books surpassed it in style, complexity and skill.

The theme of many of his novels is the effect of the 'tragic passing of time' on the human face and body, where to make this apparent in the narrative is as fundamentally necessary for a writer as it is for a painter to work in two dimensions yet give the subject life, a hurdle to be crossed before genius can develop in either medium. This was a skill Bennett acquired early on.

A chronological time scheme was synchronised to the cogs and flywheels of the plot, Time a deadly hunter pursuing its characters into all sorts of swamps, perilous situations and, at times, sunny valleys – but which corners them in the end. Bennett guides his people from the beginning of their lives to the end, as if using the tools and fire of a blacksmith to shape events on the solid anvil of time.

He had little thought of changing the form of the novel, only to push it a little beyond what had been established by his predecessors. He would enrich and even modernise, having been influenced by the French realists, but valued his genius too highly to flout the limits of tradition. Not enough of a 'genius' to put his self-confidence at risk, for which we have only the gods to thank, in *The Old Wives' Tale* he came closer to creating a work of genius than in any of his other books.

Thrust out of his natal environment by a socially impaired character, or by a poetic lust to see the whole earth and not only his birthplace, Bennett had to survive in the strange area of London, and paid for the privilege with self-destroying industry, the most enduring ability he brought with him.

Quintessentially a 'man from the North', he found his profitable seam of the literary mine and, most of the time, liked it there, becoming successful enough to enjoy his popularity, as well as sufficiently human to believe those critics who said good things of his work, and ignore whoever did not. He assumed that critics speak only for themselves, taking from novels those features that affect their own perceptions of the world, whereas a novelist speaks to everyone.

Enoch Arnold Bennett was born in 1867, near Hanley in Staffordshire. His father, a 'self-made man', did not qualify in his profession of solicitor till his mid-thirties, after prolonged study at home. There can be no more tyrannical person than one who is unaware of the tyranny in demanding that his son become a model of himself. Bennett worked in his office after leaving school for nothing more than spending money, but at 21, unknown to his father, by answering advertisements in a newspaper he secured a job in London as a lawyers' clerk. He said to one of his Burslem friends: 'Frank, I'm going to get out of this' – meaning the influence of his father, and of the Potteries. His determination to get away was not an inspired remark that popped out of nowhere, but had been there since birth and, reinforcing itself through childhood and adolescence, led him to write some of the best novels and stories of his time.

He set off for London in March 1889, at the age of 22, having already done some minor journalism for a local paper, as well as having fallen under the influence of the romantic novelist Marie Louise de la Ramée (1839–1908), who wrote under the name of Ouida.

177

Bennett had long felt the attraction of all things French, and learned some of the language as a schoolboy, regarding such knowledge as essential for an educated man. On his way to school he was told that a Frenchwoman had come to live in Burslem and, greeting her in French, as she was standing by her gate, received a smiling reply, to the admiration of his schoolmates.

For most novelists born in the provinces the move to London is a vital transition. Bennett was forced out of the Potteries by an incompatibility he could not control, the urge to leave carrying with it a buried conflict which became the powerhouse of his best work.

Just as London was the clearing house of manufacturing profits from the North, so it was also for writers and artists, to whom 'coming down south' meant being reborn, and in some ways to be a child again, such are the difficulties of a different and demanding world. A man from the provinces, brought up in an industrial town, but often within walking distance of grandiose houses and extensive parks, finds a new and invigorating existence waiting for him. In the North one lives in a town with little more than a square mile of built-up centre, from which homely zone one can reach open country on foot, whereas London stretches so hugely that the only manageable space is the distance between one's room and the Underground railway. A day must be devoted to visiting the countryside, and a place where a writer can't get easily at fields and hills is hardly worth living in. So much brick and concrete, so much foul air, and such density of people and traffic dulls the senses.

Rather than be buried alive in London it is better to go to France or Spain, for a year or two of exile, where one can also get used to the world again after leaving one's native place. Whoever does so can regain the self-confidence once possessed among the acquaintances of his own town, rise above the effects of English class feeling against the provinces, and acquire the veneer of the traveller who has imbibed the more democratic notions of the continent. The sense of superiority (ultimately dubious though it may be), which all English men feel when among the people of a different country, enable him to come back, and not only meet the English on their own terms, but feel superior to *them* as well.

Bennett regretted that he had been forced into his father's office at sixteen, and not gone on to university, so his periods of exile in France were all the more necessary. He was afflicted by a life-long stutter, and had been occasionally mocked about it by his father. School must have been difficult, but he was a robust boy who could hold his own. H G Wells thought the stutter had some sexual cause from early childhood, but it helped Bennett to become far more famous in his home town than whoever had tormented him: he not only went south, but became celebrated as well, at a time when there was a greater psychic distance between London and the Trent than exists today.

His first novel, emphasising the importance he attached to having made the break, was *A Man from the North*, published in 1898, when he was 31. Fairly well reviewed, he made a profit of one guinea, with which he went out to buy a new hat!

Joseph Conrad wrote to him: '*A Man from the North* has inspired me with the greatest respect for your artistic conscience. I am profoundly impressed with the achievement of style. The root of the matter – which is expression – is there, and the sacred fire, too. I hope you will give me the credit for understanding what you have tried for there. My dear sir, I do envy you the power of coming so near to your desire.'

Bennett lived in Chelsea and earned his living by journalism and other writings. His first visit to Paris did not come up to expectations, the effect that of an underwater delayed-action mine only to detonate on subsequent visits.

Knowing himself still very much the unsophisticated man from the North did not encourage him to stay in France, and he didn't go back for six years. In that time his father had died, he published *Anna of the Five Towns*, and at 36 years of age knew that he was approaching the height of his powers as a novelist. Sitting in a Paris restaurant one evening, close to a rather fat woman surrounded by many parcels, he noted that she wore a cloak and a 'light-puce flannel dress', and that she was one of those eccentric people who live alone, sensitive, touchy and not the sort you care to look at while eating your dinner. He thought of a story to be called 'The History of Two Old Women', in which she would have a sister, as fat as herself, who had been married to a very ordinary man and had become a widow.

The other sister had been a prostitute, but they would live together in old age. One of the waitresses in the restaurant was a beautiful pale young girl, and he saw that this fat, disagreeable woman who, affected by his unspoken dislike had gone to another table, had once been as pleasant and beautiful as she. Even before this germ of the novel occurred to him, Bennett contemplated writing an English version of Guy de Maupassant's *Une Vie* – the story of a woman's life. Yet lest he be accused of imitation, he would write about two women, who would be sisters.

He began *The Old Wives' Tale* five years later, on 8 October in 1907, at Fontainebleau, where he and his wife had rented a house for £36 a year. From 1906 to 1909 his earnings averaged eleven pounds a week, not a low income for the time, but this only after a prodigious amount of work, proof that literary reputation is often far higher than the reward. During the 1920s, however, he was happy to note that he was being paid at the rate of half-a-crown a word – yet was irked that he didn't get as much as Kipling or Eden Philpotts.

The average labourer in England, in 1906, was lucky to take home a pound a week (the equivalent of £50 in today's money) and a clerk might earn two or three. Bennett, who did much journalism in his lifetime, was obsessed with the number of words he could write in a year – so many hundred-thousand during the twelve-month, so many thousand words a day. In 1908 he was pleased to note that his output had totalled 423,500 words – at a time when his income was eleven pounds a week! Even so, he might sometimes have regretted giving up secure commissions in London, and taking to the uncertain life of a freelance abroad.

The Old Wives' Tale opens in a draper's shop overlooking the market square of Burley in the 1850s, twenty years before Bennett's birth, which makes it to some extent historical, in recreating the parsimoniousness and brutality of nnieteenth-century England, yet he imbued it with a strong flavour of romance.

The sisters grow up together. Sophia is beautiful, clever and of unpredictable temper, while her sister Constance is obedient and quiet, moulded by the traditions and wishes of her parents. Perhaps such differences formed the two basic sides of Bennett's own character, and they fought themselves out on the battleground of his novel.

Sophia's destiny takes her to Paris for thirty years, with a husband who early on abandons her to the hardship of earning a living in unfamiliar circumstances. She has to face the Franco-Prussian War, and the uncertainties of the siege by the Prussians, and the insurrection of the Commune which overwhelms Paris.

Constance in England leads an ordinary existence, with a husband who takes over the family shop. They have a child, but the humdrum life is heightened by Bennett's love of the subject. He carried a fond regard for the Potteries wherever he went, and could never resist, when out to dinner, lifting the plates to look at the familiar trademark underneath. These home pages have more life and poetry than those which cover the exciting and dangerous events in France.

Sophia and Constance come back together when they are about sixty, which Bennett considers to be old, treating them as if they were almost senile. He himself died at the fairly young age of 64, and possibly thought that old age was that at which you died, no matter how many years had been lived.

Sophia and Constance change and grow as their flesh-and-blood faces give way to time. Circumstances alter, their ideas become more fixed and even rigid, as they diverge from each other. They seem to have grown apart forever, but when they meet again each unique spirit is less fixed than had been thought, due to their common childhood. Both cease to be the distinctive personalities they had been when younger and living apart. Some critics complained that the final chapters of the novel were not so moving as those which preceded them, yet

181

the diminution of excitement is more involving by being so truthful and tragic.

Bennett was not a poet, but at times used concise and poetic imagery. Regarding telegraph lines: 'One could imagine the messages in the wires under the feet of birds.' The order of the words show his priorities, because people are moved more by prices and money (an obsession with getting bread and the good things in life) than with death and time. Horses and birds signify energy, and a freedom which is unobtainable by human beings in the hands of a fate they can't control.

Sophia's first reaction to love as a young girl: 'She was drunk; thoughts were tumbling about in her brain like cargo loose in a rolling ship.' On the ideals of her father, which went with him to the grave, Bennett observes how true it is that 'ideals die; not in the conventional pageantry of honoured death, but sorrily, ignobly, while one's head is turned.'

The realist, in these socially exact novels of the lower middle class, allows no trace of radical politics to enter – certainly not to develop. Unaware of the ideals of the Paris Commune – brutal enough, and wiped out by internecine butchery – Constance thinks only of hoarding food and, a true daughter of Victorian England, charging her boarding house guests as much as she can get away with, though she does wonder about the purpose of her sister's more ordinary existence.

Bennett covers half a century in the lives of his Midlands people, and at the end can only ask what has been the point. To live, one might have told him, in such a way that life might be a little better for those who came after, but he tells the story, and does not search for answers, except a few that pose no deeper questions. Maybe Constance could not wonder about the purpose of her as-yet unfinished life because Bennett's own was far from ended.

Bennett portrays ordinary people realistically and not as caricatures. Constance, Samuel Povey the draper's assistant, Maggie the servant, Gerald Scales, Mrs Baines – none has that whimsical aspect that tends to amuse and obscure rather than properly show what sort of people they are. He puts everyone in their place, revelling in the compartmented life of the times.

He mentioned the 'outrages' during the Reform Riots of 1832, not entirely blind to people wanting a form of human rights, and an end to constant hunger and the uncertainties of employment.

Towards the close of her life, Constance doubts for a moment the efficacy as well as the necessity of English puritan values, as if not sure that her sister's adventurous (though more tragic) life abroad was so empty after all. Other lives sometimes seem more exciting than the ones we scratch along with in our humdrum ways, but Sophia and Constance recognise stalemate in their reunion.

Bennett's attitude to the federation of the Five Towns into one agglomeration of England's 'twelfth largest city' is ironic and disapproving, but his book is, after all, an old wives' tale, showing how stay-at-homes come out better in the end than erring daughters who light off for foreign places.

Maybe there was something in this for himself. He was never sure whether or not he had done right, except in his novels, which not only earned money but became his reason for staying alive, so that he pursued his career with energy and brio to the end.

The Old Wives' Tale sold hardly any copies in the first month, until an enthusiastic review by H G Wells sent it into a modest second edition. It then began to sell steadily, due to the gathering momentum of sales in the United States, though it never became a bestseller in England during Bennett's lifetime. Perhaps it was too much like other novels of the day, and needed time to show that it stood head and shoulders above the rest.

Clayhanger (1910) had the stature of *The Old Wives' Tale* but is a more poetic novel in that the final pages are dominated by Hilda Lessways, one of his more complex female characters. He was anxious lest the reviewers compare the novel unfavourably with *The Old Wives' Tale*, unable to find much else to say, and John Galsworthy did, in fact, write to say that he preferred the former work.

Bennett never reached or searched for the chaos beneath the surface – behind a person's eyes, as it were – but he had some influence on other writers, whether they acknowledged it or not. Cyril, the hero of D H Lawrence's first novel *The White Peacock*, who has much the same aura as Constance's son Cyril in *The Old Wives' Tale*, was published three years later, and nine years after *Anna of the Five Towns*. Lawrence said that he wanted to write a novel that would do for Nottinghamshire what Bennett had done for the Potteries, and he achieved something of this in the first half of *The Lost Girl*. There is also a similarity late in that book to *The Old Wives' Tale*, where Bennett gives French conversations in a stilted, directly translated English. In *The Lost Girl* Alvina Houghton is involved in the even more linguistic folly of the Natcha-Kee-Tarawa circus troupe. Lawrence had no great respect for Bennett, the obvious influence in his early work not encouraging him to follow in his footsteps, only to point out their fundamental differences. Lawrence took himself to places far beyond London, and derided those values that Bennett, a more typical man from the North, was content to live by.

After the publication of Riceyman Steps, Wells wrote to Bennett: 'I have to join the chorus. Riceyman Steps is a great book. I hate to go back on an old friend, but I think it is as good as or better than *The Old Wives' Tale*.' Conrad was 'wholly delighted with it', and Thomas Hardy was 'absolutely absorbed by it', such writers showing a generosity that seems absent today.

The novel, about a miserly bookseller, and his servant Elsie, achieves a perfect harmony of style and story, running so smoothly that it leaves one with the feeling of having read something profoundly and completely satisfying.

By now Bennett had a country house and a yacht (with a piano on board) and could live the life of a rich man. Yet after he died there were rumours he hadn't left enough money to pay the milk bill. During his final illness the Borough Council laid straw along Marylebone Road to deaden the traffic noise.

Bennett's work could not be compared to that of the more avant-garde writers of the twenties but, at the end of broadstream English writing, he gave an accolade of respectful interest, as did D H Lawrence, to the literature that had industrial England as its background. Since Bennett's day novelists have moved from works of breadth and scale, the concept of time not being imperative. Pace changes, values alter, and wars come and go. Everything has its price, and exacts its toll.

Modern writers achieve effect by a style based on common rhythms and forms of speech, using the concept of time, in all its shifting possibilities, sometimes as a way of implying profundity and originality. Bennett's language was in the clear, straightforward manner of the nineteenth century.

In the 1960s it occasionally seemed as if the North was crowding out the South in the world of English letters, though it's hard to say why. It was as if the North was more interesting and exciting because life was harder there, the landscape more spectacular, the people less open but at the same time more friendly. The few words spoken were more vivid, so that when a young writer found the dam of self-expression broken, the words tumbled out and formed their own unique river.

Southerners were sometimes surprised that a man from the North could be a writer, especially if he hadn't been to university, and when he appeared (bog mud and iron filings adhering to his boots), his work was noticed more than many a writer from the South.

Anyone today who writes novels set in the Midlands or the North receives little attention from the Oxbridge network in control of the reviewing. A novel about ordinary and recognisable people with real problems and half-understood aspirations (and very good stories as well) is marked down as of little significance if it has a regional setting, as if the people written about are inferior and don't deserve to be used in fiction.

And even if spurned by reviewers so that their books are little bought, such writers are nevertheless much read – at least according to my yearly cheque for Public Lending Right. It is still in that respect a country of two nations. The only test of a novel is how long people go on wanting to read it.

People from the North were impregnated with the power of their landscape, and under the veneer of sophistication found it hard to forget the factory chimneys, the combs and crags, the

Severn at Ironbridge like a silvery anaconda among wooded Shropshire hills, with its half-hidden manufacturies, diseased lime kilns, disused gin-pits along sylvan valleys, the canals and their rotting lock gates, forges and foundries, tips and slag heaps and smelting works, the snow-patched seemingly endless moors in winter, and churned earth making the aftermath of the Somme battles look like the landscape for a Surrey cricket match. The scenes and life among such landscapes stay in the subconscious, as if they can neither forget nor forgive being abandoned, though today none of it exists, only the eerie tranquillity of a bygone age.

Bennett had his thousand or more words a day, his eighty books that kept him going till he was 64. And then he died of typhoid fever because, foolishly going against the advice of a waiter, he took a glass of unboiled water. 'If all the French people in Paris drink it,' he scoffed, 'what have I to fear?'

It was a pity it took him so long to realise that even in the South people know what they are talking about. One can imagine the remarks of Sophia in *The Old Wives' Tale*: 'Serves you right. In the Five Towns you can drink the tap water, but not in Paris.' A high price to pay for the youthful desertion of his birthplace; he was both victim and hero of his fate.

Robert Graves' Centenary

Every time I look at a blank sheet of paper, calling out to be covered by writing, a positively catatonic state comes over me. A blue sky out of the window, and a magical, though heavily polluted breeze wafting in, is no help. Maybe last night's vodka has dulled my mind, though a few glasses never seemed too much. I want to be parking my car in the valley of the Derwent at Matlock, and walking up the Heights of Abraham in spring, puffing my way through aromatic woods for a wonderful view from the summit.

The unfriendly neighbourhood pneumatic drill is back, two car alarms are competing for attention, and a police van goes bansheeing by. Maybe I've got a fatal illness, or it could be a cold coming on. All the same, I reflect, don't fatal illnesses usually begin by you thinking it's only a cold? More often than not, in the usual mindless drift before beginning to write something – anything – scenes from the island of Majorca float into view, where I spent much of my youth. From 1970 a gap of twenty years went by before going back, and when I did, and stepped out of the plane, it was obvious that whoever said you can't go home again didn't know what they were talking about.

I went there in 1995 to celebrate the one hundredth anniversary of the birth of Robert Graves, and on 11 November my part in it was to read some of his poems in a small church overlooking the village where he had lived most of his life.

Graves was a great poet, and an excellent novelist, but he was also an inspiration to young writers. He never discouraged anyone who called on him, or showed him their work, and was always more than generous with his time and advice. I cycled the 2 kilometres from Soller to see him in the spring of 1953, when he was busy on eight different books. But he found the time to talk to me, and also to listen, and I stayed well into the evening, cycling back in twilight along the winding Spanish road with more than a few brandies inside me. It was Robert who, a couple of years later, suggested I write a novel set in Nottingham.

To live on the island these days needs more money than the RAF pension I drew for the whole of the 1950s. A fully enough furnished five-roomed flat in Soller, with a view from the back terrace of town and the mountains behind, cost a pound a week, the equivalent of twenty today – or a hundred, if you could even find a place.

The long indented northern coast of pine forests and olive groves hadn't altered, was still unbelievably enchanting, as we were driven to our room in Richard Branson's more-than-perfect hotel in Deya, the sort of accommodation hardly dreamed of in the old times, nor in these days either if we had to pay for it ourselves.

A few days later, from a spot beneath the ornate pulpit of the church, I read six of Robert's poems. They had been difficult to choose from all he had written, but three concerned his son David, who had been killed in action in Burma during the Second World War. I somehow knew that this was what Robert would have wanted.

At eleven o'clock precisely I announced to the full church the two minutes' silence for Armistice Day. After the required standing to attention, my military posture coming back, we filed outside, to lay a wreath sent by officers of Robert's old regiment, The Royal Welch Fusiliers. It was an apt symbol for an ex-soldier and a great writer, its cluster of Flanders poppies comfortable within a circlet of rich green. Robert's widow Beryl led us through the cemetery gate, to place it beneath the simple headstone.

Hard to say who had it in for whom, but the weather in Majorca is unpredictable at that season, and no sooner was the wreath where it should have been than a rogue wind swooped from nowhere and sent it flying away. The younger men in the congregation scaled the walls, chased it downhill, and in a few minutes brought it back, though in their wisdom didn't lay it down again until the wind had slunk away to its cave at dusk. Beryl thought that Robert, wherever he was, must have had a hand in the wreath's whirligig escapade, to amuse himself at our expense.

During the next few days I was still in thrall to the island where, sitting under an orange tree, I began to write *Saturday Night and Sunday Morning*. Perhaps having left such a paradise was just one more mistake in my life. Every decision is a door with a thousand hinges, and it makes no noise when you so blithely open it and pass through.

Call it Fate, or fear, or lack of perception, or what you will, because I am back in London with a blank page before me, though I needn't castigate myself for being idle because I have a novel about to be published, and one already finished for next year.

The greatest of French writers, Stendhal, said: 'In England a man might be half a moron, and still write a passable book.' Thank you very much, Henri, but my pen is starting to move across the blank page, and I have no option but to follow. My father's response, when I expressed a reluctance at fourteen to go down to the factory and get a job was: 'No work, no food' – a brevity I only appreciated on becoming a writer. Certain it is, though, that thoughts of Majorca never fail to inspire.

Ted Hughes, by Alan Sillitoe

The coffin in which Ted lay, on the floor below the pulpit in North Tawton church, seemed huge, far, too big and heavy to be carried on human shoulders, but the pall bearers did their job and lifted it, slow marched up the aisle to the music of Elgar's 'Nimrod' – a fitting tune for a hunter before the Lord. This was the only part of the service at which I felt that tears might come, because now it was more than obvious that he couldn't be anything but dead, the body at least out of everyone's life forever.

It was always my notion that Ted would have been writing some kind of obituary for me, but these days God seems to have his hands on a machine gun, and is no respecter of a few odd years between contemporaries. Why he should have gone first I'll never know.

When I received the Hawthornden Prize for *The Loneliness of the Long Distance Runner* it was the custom that the winner would be present at the ceremony for whoever was awarded it the following year. This happened to be Ted Hughes, for *The Hawk in the Rain*, and we met on the steps of a house in St James's Square, in the summer of 1961, which makes him one of my oldest friends.

Sylvia Plath was there, as was Ruth Fainlight (our wives), both poets and American. Ted and myself were (though it's stretching the point for me) from 'the North', and in the following weeks we ate dinner in each others' flats. Ruth and I must have been among the first to call on them when they bought Court Green in Devon a couple of months later.

Ted was diffident and modest, even taciturn, but what enlivened our gatherings was a sense of humour, laughter taking up almost as much time as speech, as if we were plugged into the same rich vein. In 1962 Ruth Fainlight and myself went to Tangier for the year with our baby son David, and at the end of that time, after Ted and Sylvia had split up, Ruth arranged to stay with her for a month while I was in Russia. Tragically, Sylvia killed herself, and we often wonder whether she would have done so, had we been in England. Suicides deserve pity, but they have much to answer for.

Our friendship with Ted lasted. One night at Court Green, sometime in the seventies, we sat at table with his sister, Olwyn, deploring the fact that poetry publications weren't cheaper and more widely available. Wondering what to do about it, we spent the time over several bottles and a long dinner working out details of *The Giveaway Press*. Poems would be printed on the cheapest of paper and sold on street corners for only a penny or two. The result, after a couple of years, (and we later laughed about it) was *The Rainbow Press*, each plush, boxed volume costing about £75!

On another convivial evening Ted and I worked out the logistics of a trip to the beaches of Gallipoli. His father had been an infantryman there in 1915, and had told Ted that the winnings of a pontoon school among the troops, amounting to several hundred sovereigns, had been buried in the sand and must still be there. We opened maps and reckoned up distances, calculated the number of days to drive there, and the supplies to take. That plan did not materialise either, all of us having more important things to do.

Ted retreated more and more into himself as the years went by, which was understandable, but to me he wasn't the silent ox-like and morose creature people imagine. The closeness and rapport remained, in that he always sent copies of his books to me, and I reciprocated with copies of mine, both offering comments in our letters. In later years we could be relied on to leave each other alone because, as Ted wrote in a letter: 'As you get older, guarding your time has to be the greatest aim', as indeed it always had been and still is with me.

On 1 January 1997 he called at our place in Somerset on his way to London with Roy Davids. In those two or three hours the mood was as open and free as at any time before. Why he was going to London we didn't know, though it obviously had something to do with his illness, about which I had only heard rumours.

Whatever it was, he wouldn't tell, being reticent about such things, but I didn't imagine, as we waved him off, that it was the last time I'd see him.

To St Catherine's Monastery

On 26 July 1977, just after half-past five in the morning, we headed for the Dead Sea. Free of the conurbation of Jerusalem, though not before we had stopped to buy a few flat loaves of delicious Arab bread, the road made wide sweeping curves through the wilderness of Judaea. Moab in Jordan isn't usually visible in summer, nor was it now, and a seven-tenths strato-cumulus persisted nearly to Jericho, at which level we were slightly cooler, the barometer having dropped from 2,600 feet above the sea to a thousand feet below. The usual stench of sulphur met us along the shore of the Dead Sea.

David, our fifteen-year-old son, sighted a Tristram's grackle at En Gedi, attracted by its forlorn Holy Land hoot, a *gracula* of the Palestinian sort first noted by the Reverend Tristram on his travels in 1863–4. We had already tried to track one down at the Monastery of Maa-Saba, but only heard them among the rocks.

We gave a soldier a lift as far as Eilat, difficult as this was with our luggage, but he couldn't be left behind. During our three months in Israel we must have shifted a good proportion of the army, both men and women, with their firearms and radio gear.

Desolation was total, the air sultry after passing Massada, with acres of salt pans and pyramids of rock, the landscape eroded like flaky pastry created by a cook gone mad. The idea was to call at Sodom, at the southern end of the sea, and send postcards to friends, but we missed the place entirely, because there was nothing to mark it, and certainly not a post office.

It was arid all the way, until at half-past ten we drove over a hill and saw ships in the port of Eilat, our journey from London by car bringing us within sight of Arabia across the gulf. Little of interest in the town, we talked to a woman at the tourist office, who said that the road to St Catherine's Monastery was impossible for ordinary cars.

'Even a robust Peugeot Estate?' We'd seen the saloon equivalents in films, slithering all over the tracks of East Africa.

'I'm afraid so,' she smiled.

In an undersea aquarium south of the town, fish of all the rainbows flitted beyond the windows. Our nightstop was at Neviot, a palm grove by the beach, where one could camp between the trees and bushes. A man went by on a camel, one of the Bedouins from their nearby settlement. Mountains formed a jagged line inland, the main Sinai range coming down almost to the sea.

After putting up our tent I made tea, with sugar and powdered milk. The wind from the sea was cool, but when the sun descended behind the crestline the air turned warm and sultry, the wind then coming from inland, though at times it seemed to blow from all directions at once. I swam, but the water was shallow for a long way out. Maybe the Israelis could reclaim the land, I thought, canalise the Gulf of Eilat and create a belt of fertility along the shore.

At dusk lights went on at the nearby *moshav*. After supper an Israeli couple sent a boy over with a bottle of ice-cold water from their refrigerator. When we called to thank them, giving their son a Jubilee Crown as a souvenir, they opened a bottle of wine. It was safe to camp anywhere in Sinai, they said. The Bedouins work for the government of Israel, as they always have for whoever ruled their territory.

Drinking so much wine, as well as the heat of the night, stopped me getting to sleep for an hour or so. I bedded down in the car, at three in the morning saw the baleful eyes of a camel staring through the windscreen, one of several plodding up and down the beach searching for leftovers from picnics.

At five I got up and ran into the refreshing water, then brewed tea. The usual brilliant and scorching day. Campers woke and made themselves comfortable. We should have brought a washing-up bowl instead of the sextant, an extra jerry can for water instead of the short-wave radio, and a luggage rack to carry a proper tent big enough for the three of us, as well as a folding table and a couple of chairs.

Feeling better than for years, as I often did when on the road, I drove inland through a pass. A wide ascending wadi, ashy and without habitation, was flanked by sharp-edged purple and grey mountains. Bedouins tramped their camels in the distance, as if from our smooth road of black silk we were looking on at them from another planet.

Back to the sea at Dahab, we had breakfast of sausage, olives and hard-boiled eggs, among kiosks and picnic shelters by the beach. A hot and irritating wind blew grit in hair and eyes, curtailing our meal. A Bedouin girl was letting out a rather moth-eaten dromedary for short rides and photographs.

Once more into desolation upon desolation, range beyond jagged range, grey and reddish, then slowly becoming separate peaks surrounded by sand, as Alpine mountains are lapped and enclosed with snow. But the snow was pink with a blue sheen to it, and a haze overhead that tired the eyes.

Seeing a lake in the distance I stopped to check its position on the map, but it was a deception, a mirage no less, a sheet of water slowly dissolving as the car went on. David slept for fifty miles. A young hitch-hiker picked up at Dahab got out at the settlement of Ophira. At the youth hostel it was said that a family room would be available for us from five o'clock.

The direct road from the Ras Mohammed Nature Reserve was closed because of military installations, so instead of twelve kilometres I drove thirty west and another thirty back to get there. The track was unpaved, sand beaten into hard ribs by the action of the wind, which rattled the car like an old boneshaker.

The southern-most point of Israel looked out across rocks and the sheer blue of the Red Sea, nothing between us and the

Straits of Aden and the Indian Ocean. Mr Ram, the director of the nature reserve, gave David permission to collect insects from the mangrove swamp – the most northerly and probably therefore the most interesting one in the world. When back in London the British Museum of Natural History took three hundred specimens he had collected in similar remote parts of the country.

Back in Ophira, the mountains stood out in the dusk, rising stark and reddish, as if I could put out my hands, lift them from their ponds and pools of sand, and crumble them into dust. In the later light of afternoon they seemed made of cardboard, one panorama slid in front of another, going back north into the main body of the Sinai Peninsula.

After my cold shower and shave – a temporary cure for exhaustion – we had supper in the hostel dining room. I asked again about the road to the monastery, and the director of the hostel, Jacob Bar-Levy, said he thought it might, after all, be possible to get there in our sort of car. He had left Haifa five months before to take up his job here, having given up a career in engineering.

At eight-thirty I filled up at the petrol station, then called at the supermarket, which stocked whatever a traveller might want, though all we needed was a bar of soap. A sixty-year-old American writer who lived in Rome, called Waller, asked for a lift as far as Ras Mohammed.

The route was littered with rusty lorries, spiked guns and smashed half-tracks, all pointing north, blasted by aircraft in the Egyptian rout of 1967. At the United Nations demarcation line I suspected we had overshot our turning, and confirmed it by a compass bearing, so I turned back to find the right place.

We picked up the same young man we had given a lift to the day before, who told us he had slept on the beach at Ras Mohammed. We gave him water, which he badly needed. On getting into the car he seemed doubtful whether it was sturdy enough for the road ahead, but decided to take his chance. Seventeen years old, he came from a kibbutz near Rehovot, supposedly on holiday with friends in Eilat, but he had decided to hitch-hike to the monastery.

A couple of crew-cut Germans, who had driven their jeep all the way from Dortmund, followed us for a while, imagining we knew the way better than they did. The inconspicuous signposts were in Hebrew, but I had learned to decipher the alphabet before leaving London. Place names on the map sheet were also in Hebrew, the map not very clearly printed, and tending to fall to pieces if opened too often.

Turning inland I began a hard five-hour drive of 130 kilometres to a height of 4,500 feet. The gradual ascent took us along wadi beds, in some places several miles wide, bordered by jagged mauve ridges and grey peaks. The surface was mostly gravel and sand, and it was impossible to go fast. A great clatter as the car hit concealed rocks made me fear that a sharp-edged stone might slit the petrol tank like the iceberg that ripped open the belly of the *Titanic*, or cut all four tyres to shreds so that we would be stranded. One had to concentrate every metre of the way. Now and again we stopped to snack and drink, and for David to get to work with his geological hammer. Several weighty specimens in plastic bags were labelled and loaded into the car.

Feiran, the only inhabited spot, was a walled oasis with thickly packed palm groves. It had been a bishopric in the fourth century, and now the Israeli government had opened schools and clinics. It was here that the Ancient Israelites defeated the Amalekites, who tried to dispute their passage to the Promised Land after the Exodus from Egypt.

The air was fresh and the sky clear on the high ground by St Catherine's Monastery. There were one or two houses for local people, some scattered buildings belonging to the monastery, and a petrol station. The area had opened out somewhat since Israel took it over in 1967. The monastery itself was a red-walled imposing fortress, but we had no hope of getting in. The driver of a desert bus told us it had been closed some weeks ago because the monks were overwhelmed by the number of tourists. They were unsympathetic to the Israeli government for opening the

Field Studies School; the priests had also lost the goodwill of the local people, who now earned more by working for the Israelis.

We drove across the plateau to a café, and sat on the veranda drinking cups of muddy but refreshing coffee. David spotted a pair of Tristram's grackles perched on a camel, after hearing their unmistakably mournful sound. The Germans drove up in their jeep, looking as if we had let them down by shooting on ahead after Feiran. They asked where the camp site was, and I had to tell them I didn't know. We had no idea where we were going to sleep either, but hoped to get accommodation at the Field Studies School.

A cable loose under the car explained why the speedometer hadn't been working since Feiran. With the connection broken, I would neither know my speed on the road, nor how far we were from point to point, but since speed could be estimated, and distances calculated from the map, this wasn't a serious matter. I only hoped nothing else would come apart on the way back. The building, with its interior court, resembled a khan on the road to Llasa, high peaks surrounding the square low walls of mountain stone. A full moon glowed like a stationary cannonball overhead, and Ursa Major was brilliantly delineated.

We were up before six, to a clear sky and perfectly outlined mountains, the usual cardboard cutouts one behind the other. From a dip in the jagged rock a reflection of orange light from the sun shone on another range behind.

Tea was made, and the bunks tidied. A row of taps in the open air served for ablutions, with a steel trough to take the water away. I stood to shave at the single cracked mirror, between a couple of busty and handsome girls from the Field Studies School.

The petrol station was said to open at seven, but the Arab attendant came a minute or two before, and got the donkey engine thumping to start the pumps. While unlocking each one the engine failed, so had to be set going again. However, we were off down the valley by half-past seven, the way now easy to find, so that instead of five hours to reach the paved road we got there in just over three, because I was also more experienced in tackling the rough terrain. The idea was to go at the washboard effect at

198

fifty miles an hour, instead of twenty, the car thus suffering less from vibration, or so I hoped.

Nevertheless, on hitting the occasional rock I feared for the radio and navigation instruments, as well as other delicate pieces of luggage. But we belted along, swerving sometimes to avoid plain obstacles, and in places gliding above deep gravel ruts. One of the rear mudguard flaps dropped off, but I went on with the tiring yet exhilarating ride. A patch of smashed melons and a few score broken eggs must have dropped off a lorry, and we also passed ragged tyres and a burnt-out jeep.

A mile or two after Feiran, a Greek Orthodox priest wearing a tall black hat leaned out of his Lancia car to ask if the archbishop was up at the monastery. I told him we'd had no way of finding out. 'Do you think this car's good enough for the road ahead?' he wanted to know, giving a fine wide smile. I said I supposed it was, since ours had already come that way and it didn't really get much worse, at which he drove off quite merrily.

Half-past ten, the rally track behind us, Ruth took the wheel as far as Ophira. On the way she was signalled to the roadside and asked if we would take two youths on board. They had started hitch-hiking to the monastery but had almost succumbed for lack of water and now felt there was little possibility of crossing any more desert. So space was made, till they could be let out at Ophira.

Before turning north, a stop was made at Ras Nasrani, from which headland Egyptian guns once controlled the straits of Tiran. After Neviot darkness came on, the moon shining over Jordan, precipitous mountains showing below as well as above the water.

After our 500-kilometre run we dropped into a comfortable room at the Moon Valley Hotel in Eilat. The buffet provided a cold dinner, welcome after mainly snacks during the last few days. Dead beat by ten o'clock, we turned in.

First thing on getting up was to have a refreshing swim in the hotel pool, then a Lucullan breakfast of salt fish, cheese, hard-boiled eggs, butter, tomatoes, peppers, olives, cream cheese, fresh bread and coffee etc. etc. – which was gorged on till no more would go in. We picked up a rather sullen-looking Yemenite sort of girl soldier, who wanted to go to Beer Sheba. A soldier by the pick-up stop asked us to take him and his girlfriend as well, but only one passenger could be fitted in comfortably. The quick-witted Yemenite girl summed up the situation, threw in her pack, got into the empty back seat, and we were off. The soldier's shirt was open, as if he had slept outside, and the yellow word *zahal* proved him a soldier, though I wondered if he was serving at the moment. Some, I suppose, keep their shirts after leaving the army and wear them to hitch around in because it is easier to get lifts, though everyone is an ex-serviceman or woman in Israel.

Beyond Gerofit we turned onto the road through the Negev desert, passing some gypsum mine workings, pyramids of white powder for making plaster of Paris. Below the great escarpment, not far from Mizzpah Ramon, a lorry had gone over the cliff and, today being the Sabbath, an effort was being made to get it up with two mobile cranes. It was a slow job. Our car and many others were stopped on the slope, so I wedged stones under the back wheels to prevent slippage.

It had been broadcast on the radio that morning that the road would be blocked, but neither we nor a dozen or so other motorists had heard it. Someone said that the driver in the lorry jumped clear, sending the truck over deliberately so as to claim the insurance, but I imagine it's a common remark in such cases. The panorama of cliffs and isolated mounds were like a geological layer cake, though visibility, as always, was not perfect in such heat.

The girl soldier left us, because an army lorry on the other side was taking people on to the town. I put a sheet over our windscreen to keep off the extreme heat, though there was something of a breeze. Fat-bellied black-and-white crag martins performed aerobatics from the cliff face, weaving into space to do their stuff.

The barometer showed 2,430 feet, and close by, along the road and just beyond and above the blockage, coming down a 250-foot cliff, a stream of water made a picturesque and wispy waterfall – the sewer outlet, we were told, from Mizpah Ramon. It descended over the road and down into a wadi for miles across the baked land, a snake of green where bushes and plants had grown from the benefit of the town's conveniences.

I brought out the stove to make tea, filling the flask and a couple of pots. In the next car but one down the queue was a Dutch family of man and wife, and two boys of five and ten years old. The man came towards me and asked if I could spare some 'cooked water' for the ten-year-old in the back of his car, suffering from an upset stomach after drinking 'uncooked water' at Massada.

I filled his beaker, and added sugar, saying he was welcome, and that if he needed more he was to come back for it. He'd been in Israel for three weeks, he said, touring in a hired car. His son liked my brew so I gave him some more, and filled the inner cup of my thermos for his wife – which I omitted to get back because the electrification of a start went through the queue when the lorry was suddenly hauled onto the road and towed away. I threw stove, kettle, teapot, sugar, milk and tea into the back so as not to hold up the others.

The landscape changed near Dimona, groves of trees more frequent, a railway line to the right. A young soldier taken on board as far as Beer Sheba had circular scars up one arm, some not yet healed, and I wondered whether they were wounds, or the result of some ritual.

The man who served us at the petrol station in Beer Sheba spoke Spanish, as we did, and told us he came from Argentina. The town was almost deserted on the Sabbath, and we sat outside to have coffee because monkey-bongo music from inside the café was too loud to talk against. The proprietor who served us also spoke Spanish, and gave directions to Abraham's Well.

We were back in Patriarchs' Country, but it was closed off behind iron gates, with its concrete head put there fifty years ago. At the British War Cemetery the record book was missing. I counted twenty rows of graves with forty-five headstones in each, making over a thousand killed in the attack against the Turks in November 1917. The grass, green and freshly cut, was well cared for. Many of the dead were Australians, with touching messages from home carved on the stones. Some were Jewish, with inscriptions in Hebrew, while others had words of remembrance in Welsh. It was hard to say how long they would last, for many inscriptions were cracked or faded, so difficult to read.

At the Hebron turn-off I gave a soldier a lift to Jerusalem. The road curved up and down through pastoral country, into the hills of Judaea, some fields bare but many ploughed, an occasional large Arab village looking very prosperous. Beyond Hebron madcap drivers overtook with little space to spare on sharp bends, so I slowed down with my precious load.

Back at Mishkenot Sha'ananim, where we had a flat, thanks to Teddy Kollek, we unloaded our jumble of luggage and equipment. David noticed that he had left his briefcase in Eilat, so we phoned the hotel, to hear they'd already found it and would send it up on the next bus. It contained the complete set of his dissecting equipment, as well as a rare copy of *Animal Life in Palestine* (1935), given to him by the novelist Binyamin Tammuz.

Colonel Patterson the Zionist

Driving from Jerusalem, through the arid summer hills of Judaea, one soon reaches the flat area of the Jordan Valley. The fact that this is over a thousand feet below sea level is apparent only in the increase of heat. Beyond Jericho the land appears level, but is cut up here and there by ravines, some narrow but others hundreds of yards wide. The invisible course of the Jordan runs in a sinuous cleft to the East, and the mountains of Gilead in Jordan, faced by the escarpment-like walls of Shiloh in Israel, are twelve miles away, a cleft in the earth that goes all the way down to and almost through Africa.

Such landscape brought to mind a footnote in the *Official History of the Great War in Palestine*, which said that Colonel Patterson, the commander of the Jewish battalions in that campaign, had written a book that was 'controversial'.

Wanting to know why it was so described, some time later I bought two volumes of Patterson's war memoirs in order to find out, if I could. The first book told of the formation of the Zion Mule Corps, in Alexandria, in 1915. Lieutenant-Colonel Patterson enrolled five hundred Jews, a number of whom had fled from Palestine when Turkey entered the war on the side of Germany.

The Zion Mule Corps, with five British and eight Jewish officers, and 750 mules, landed at Gallipoli on the evening of 27 April 1915. The corps was armed with rifles captured after the unsuccessful Turkish attack on the Suez canal. Many of the men were of Russian nationality and, wrote Patterson: 'strongly desired to band themselves together into a fighting host and place their lives at the disposal of England, whom the Jews have recognised as their friend and protector from time immemorial'. They did vital work under fire, taking supplies and ammunition to infantry and gunners in the line. The bridgehead was so narrow, and shallow, that there was no safe rear area, and they shared the same peril and privations as everybody else.

After the failure of that campaign the Zion Mule Corps returned to Alexandria and was disbanded. Colonel Patterson was given command of a battalion of the Royal Dublin Fusiliers, from which post in Ireland he was summoned by telegram to the War Office on 27 July 1917, to organise and train a Jewish Legion. His book *With the Zionists in Gallipoli* had already been published, so it was fitting that he should be chosen to command a regiment composed solely of Jewish soldiers, who would eventually be sent to fight against the Turks and their German advisers.

The real mover behind the formation of the Jewish battalions, however, was Vladimir Jabotinsky who, when the war began, produced a newspaper in Copenhagen at his own expense and sent it to Jews all over the world, in which he extolled the Allied – and especially the British – cause. He then came to London and advocated the formation of Jewish military units in England and Egypt with the idea that they be used help to push the Turks out of Palestine, and so earn their right in the eyes of the world to establish a Jewish state there.

He joined the 20th Battalion of the London Regiment as a private soldier, and gathered around him a platoon of men who had served under Colonel Patterson in the Zion Mule Corps. From his position in the ranks he wrote to the prime minister, secretaries of state for war and to influential people in America, Russia and Poland, with the object not only of getting the British government to sanction the formation of a Jewish Legion, but of guaranteeing recruits to the number of fifty thousand, should this permission be given.

Colonel Patterson and Sergeant Jabotinsky met for the first time in a room at the War Office, and talked about how best to organise and train their soldiers.

On 23 August 1917 the formation of the Jewish Regiment was announced in the *London Gazette*. After training, and before departure for Palestine, five hundred men of the 38th Battalion came to London and were billeted in the Tower during the night of 3 February. The following morning – Jabotinsky was now a lieutenant – they marched with fixed bayonets through the East End, preceded by the band of the Coldstream Guards. The Star of David and the Union Jack were carried side by side, and Jewish banners greeted them along the route.

'Such a thing as a Jewish unit,' Patterson wrote, 'had been unknown in the annals of the world for some two thousand years – since the days of the Maccabees, those heroic sons of Israel who fought so valiantly, and for a time so successfully, to wrest Jerusalem from the grasp of the Roman legions.'

In order to best look after his men when they got to Egypt, Patterson assumed himself to be as Jewish as they were. While under his care he made sure, as far as was possible, that they had kosher food, and that their religious feelings were not offended in any way. He ate the same food, attended their services, and spoke of them to others as 'we Jews'.

Not much information is available about John Henry Patterson, but we know that he was born in 1867, in Northern Ireland, that he was trained as an engineer, and that on 1 March 1898 he went to East Africa as chief engineer on the Mombassa-Nairobi railway.

At a place called Tsavo the construction gangs were plagued by man-eating lions, and no less than 28 people had been eaten alive. With great skill and courage Patterson hunted and finally killed the two animals responsible, and work on the railway was resumed. Eight years later he described how he had stalked and killed the animals, which took several weeks, in his first book *The Man Eaters of Tsavo*.

He was no 'writer' but, with the engineer's eye for landscape, and attention to detail, as well as, it must be said, numerous topical clichés, but with absolute unselfconsciousness, he told an enthralling story.

He served three years in the South African War, reaching the rank of lieutenant-colonel within eight months, to be given command of the 33rd Imperial Yeomanry. Mentioned in Despatches three times, he won the Queen's Medal, and was awarded the DSO.

Before the First World War he travelled as a big game hunter, explorer and lecturer, and returned several times to East Africa on safari. In 1909 he published his second book, *In the Grip of the Nyika*. On one hunting trip he met Theodore Roosevelt, who was said to have remarked, during one of their long conversations that 'anyone who persecutes the Jews will eventually be punished.'

Patterson was fifty years old when he took command of the Jewish regiment. Any problems with his battalion in England were easily dealt with, he said, but it was different when he reached Egypt and took his all-Jewish force into Palestine. He met with billeting and dietary difficulties, and occasionally with plain racial antagonism from the staff of the Egyptian Expeditionary Force, whom he referred to as 'troublers of Israel', adding that they went out of their way to make life hard for him and his men. He did not attach much importance to it at this stage however, although, as he remarked in his book on Gallipoli, 'my temperament is not such that I suffer fools gladly.'

In August 1918 his battalion took over part of the dangerously exposed left flank of the British line in the Jordan Valley. An opposing Turkish army of ten thousand men and seventy guns was commanded by Von Falkenhayn.

Patterson's troops were part of Chaytor's Force, which consisted mainly of Australians and New Zealanders, and he makes the point that, compared to his men's treatment in other quarters, 'We had compensations in the fair, just, and kindly treatment meted out to us by General Chaytor and every officer, non-commissioned officer, and man of the Anzac Mounted Division. If we acquitted ourselves like men and performed our duties like good soldiers, then it did not matter, even if we were Jews.'

Life, even apart from the hazards of war, could be hellish. 'All day long, the sun beat down mercilessly on them, their only shelter being a flimsy bit of bivouac canvas, and the nights were stifling. Perspiration streamed from every pore, even when resting. Flies and mosquitoes deprived everyone of sleep, for our mosquito nets soon became torn and worthless, and could not be replaced.'

'Water could only be obtained in very limited quantities; every drop had to be carried from the Auja four or five miles away. The whole place was constantly enveloped in stagnant dust, so it can be imagined with what appetite a man could tackle food under such appalling conditions, every mouthful of which was necessarily full of sand and grit.'

On 2 September, when the Turks had been pushed back over the Jordan, Patterson was given command of both Jewish battalions, which were known as 'Patterson's Column'. After the fighting he received a telegram of congratulations on the excellent performance of his unit from Theodore Roosevelt, and also from General Chaytor.

Their subsequent history makes a sadder tale. Patterson had found from early on that, with regard to his men, the policy adopted by the Egyptian Expeditionary Force staff under Allenby – who, from his initial coolness towards Jewish aspirations in Palestine, seemed later to take a more favourable view – went against the officially stated intentions of the government in London. After the armistice, and before the battalions were disbanded, a reign almost of persecution was unleashed on them.

In *With the Judaeans in the Palestine Campaign* Patterson tells how, in April 1920, Arab mobs were let loose against the Jewish quarter of Jerusalem, while British troops stood by, and prevented Jewish self-defence groups from protecting their own people. Lieutenant Jabotinsky and a score of other Jews were arrested on a charge of 'rioting', and Jabotinsky was sentenced to fifteen years' penal servitude for trying to prevent what he saw as a Russian-style pogrom under British rule.

Three days of outrage went on with – as Patterson saw it – the connivance of Allenby's staff. Certain officials, he observed, treated the Balfour Declaration as if it were 'a scrap of paper'. It was Patterson's belief that these anti-Zionist activities of the military government, which he rightly saw as anti-Semitism, bore much responsibility for the enmity between the Jewish and Arab inhabitants of Palestine in the following decades.

His sense of 'fair play' was shattered, and he went home to write the book that was later referred to as 'controversial' in the official history.

Jabotinsky was released from prison shortly after his sentence, since news of the Jerusalem disturbances caused a scandal on reaching England. The military governor was replaced by Sir Herbert Samuel, and for a time things were quiet. Patterson wrote no more books, but continued to support Zionism. With his wife he helped to promote the work of the Palestine Foundation Fund in England and the United States. During the Second World War he continually pleaded with the War Office for another Jewish army, and wrote articles criticising British policies in Palestine.

He died at the age of eighty, in California, at which time he was serving as honorary chairman of the American League For a Free Palestine. Like his life-long friend Jabotinsky, he did not live to see the creation of the State of Israel, in which he had believed so long. It was plain, however, that the men who served in his battalions never forgot him. And it is certainly possible that those who stayed in Palestine put his military instruction to some use. One should refer to the tribute paid him by Jabotinsky in *The British Jewry Book of Honour, 1922*.

The fact that a man such as Patterson is singled out for praise just because he did only what was right reflects badly on those round about, who did very much less and worse. When not actually considering attitudes and conditions at the time however, one must, like Jabotinsky, give praise where it is due. Perhaps one day such distinctions will be unnecessary by their very ordinariness.

Galilee Days

I feel easy in Israel, as if I lived here as a child and have come home again, but the first week with a car I thought every minute behind the wheel would be my last, until I got used to the traffic and began to enjoy the cut and thrust. This morning, with Ruth and David, I'm on the motorway from Tel Aviv, and pass through Haifa just after eleven. We drink cups of foul coffee at a service station halfway to Akko (Acre).

I find a parking space by the ramparts. Breakers from the blue sea punch against Crusader rocks, and boys dive from a twenty-foot stump of wall into the water. Vandalism in the old town adds to occasional squalor. A water fountain had been smashed, also a public convenience. Maybe the inhabitants don't like outsiders.

The Khan Oumdan, an ancient hostelry with an enormous courtyard, has rooms below for servants and horses, and galleries above for gentlemen and, presumably, richer pilgrims. There's plenty to see, but we've been here before, and the heat makes us want to push on.

We swig coffee, buy food from a grocery shop, and set off north. I pull onto the beach for a picnic lunch near a youth hostel at Nahariya, where many people are bathing. The old customs post marking the Lebanese frontier is visible on the mountainous headland beyond, and there's something reassuring about the compact silhouette of a gunboat anchored off the coast, because the area south of Nahariya, where we are, was raided recently by Arab terrorists.

Going inland, we give a lift to a soldier, who tells us that if we take the next turning – as we intend to – we won't get beyond Adamit. But we go nevertheless, to find out what's happening along the border. The narrow paved road is deserted, with a high double fence to the left. At a bend in the road several soldiers are manning a powerful telescope, to observe fighting between Christians and Moslems. I suppose they are sensitive to signals for assistance from the former. It is ironic (to say the least) that Israel should be helping Christians after all they have suffered from them throughout history.

The post commander gesticulates angrily from an eminence above the road, indicating that we should take our Peugeot Estate car out of the area with all possible alacrity, and leave him to do his job. So we drive back 8 kilometres, hearing artillery fire much of the way, and take a parallel route further south to resume our easterly push.

The meandering road still touches the border in some places, but we stop at a petrol station outside Zefat (Safed) to fill the tank. Backtracking a few kilometres, I take the road towards Metulla along a 750-metre ridge, which gives spectacular views of the fertile Hula Valley, pestilential swamp fifty years ago. We can see Mount Hermon, and the wall of the Golan Heights, only 35 miles or three minutes' flying time from the coast. The settlements of Kfar Blum and Neot Mordekhay stand out, as well as patterns of extensive fish farms.

At half-past five, after a day's drive of 250 kilometres, which seems more than enough, a series of hairpin bends leads us to Kfar Giladi. Expecting a youth hostel family room at the kibbutz, the guest house manager puts us into a comfortable three-bed apartment. Who are we to argue?

In the dining room we choose the meat menu instead of the milk, and enjoy our four-course meal. It is a typical hotel dining room, everybody fresh from a shower, or a siesta, or a stroll (perhaps all three) and talking about their day's travels, while above the hubbub comes the unmistakable bark of artillery and the thump of bombs from beyond the nearby border, sounds giving a somewhat edgy atmosphere.

Wake at six out of solid sleep, and after breakfast walk along the shady and fragrant paths of the kibbutz. Above the warbling of doves a mixture of artillery, mortars and heavy machine-gun fire can be heard, plus a few bigger bangs from the north-west. Strange, that bombardment can be so close to this bucolic holiday atmosphere, people being killed or injured perhaps, as if we're here under the auspices of a travel firm called War Tours Inc. With the air conditioning on in the room, however, the conflict can hardly be heard.

The nearby museum of Tel Hay (The Hill of Life) is built on the scene of the last stand of Joseph Trumpeldor and his seven companions against Arab marauders in 1920. Born in Russia, Trumpeldor was decorated by the Empress after his heroic conduct at the siege of Port Arthur in the Russo-Japanese War of 1904–5, in which he lost his left arm. In 1914 he joined the Zion Mule Corps of Jewish volunteers commanded by Colonel Henry Patterson, and saw service at Gallipoli.

At Banyas, an embowered spot among streams of running water, near the source of the River Jordan, barbecues are set up, and transistor radios are on the go, so we drive from the crowd to Nimrod's Castle, an extensive ruin of crumbling walls 2,475 feet above sea level. Though in places overgrown with bushes, it is one of the best preserved in Israel, erected by the Crusaders in 1139. Nimrod, 'the mighty hunter before the Lord', was said to have been the first to build a fortress on this spot, hence its name.

A nineteenth-century silence encloses the place – no other tourists, the scenery reminiscent of a David Roberts illustration. Small black-and-white cattle wander over the stones, and a padded donkey gives its prolonged and pathetic brays, like the golden ass of Apuleius. A pair of Phantom jets, navigation lights winking, bank over the Golan Heights and descend towards Lebanon. The light brown hills are speckled by large patches of low-treed thinnish woods. The sound of exploding bombs comes from beyond Kfar Giladi.

By the ruins, at a neatly laid out stall of apples and sunflower seeds, is a young Druze with fair hair, wearing trousers and a jersey shirt. He is blind, and I suppose sits all day and every day by his wares, his only companion a middle-aged man who owns the donkey (and maybe the cattle) wearing a round white rimless hat and black clothes. Perhaps the young man is his son. They call out loudly as if to catch the attention of a third – but to us invisible – person in the area.

We continue up the flank of Mount Hermon, the paved road running through the settlement of Newe Ativ, with a gate at the entrance and one at the exit. Sloping roofs give an Alpine aspect to the place, which it must become in winter, at this elevation. The ascending road is eventually blocked by knife-switches, and though there is enough space to get the car through, I decide not to risk it, but to take a chair on the ski lift to the summit.

It felt a hazardous and fragile way of ascent, none of us having done it before. Ruth gets into the first chair, David and me on the one behind, a string of chairs going up, no one else on line, a slow and gentle ride nevertheless. The remains of T34 tanks are scattered among jagged grey rocks as if they had been mauled and broken up by some colossal being from outer space. The sky is entirely blue – a painting of Holy Land silence, no movement on the ashy desolation of rocks. It's very hot, and takes about twenty minutes to reach the permanent concrete construction at the top, where one can eat, and buy postcards and have coffee.

The terrace – the highest point of Israel and giving an unexampled view of the entire northern part of the country – is fitted with a telescope. According to the map the height is 2,224 metres. My barometer-altimeter, with a limit of 5,000 feet, has blown its top. Crowds come in winter for skiing, but there are few in midsummer. The thumping of machine-gun fire erupts from beyond the skyline, and after the echoes have died away there is silence.

Back on the chairs, we descend to the car for a picnic lunch. A valley opens far below, a large circular area, dark green in the middle, towards which moves a much-scattered flock of sheep, a shepherd walking with them. The cinematic helicopter view of the whole flock converging from one quadrant of the circle shows as so many white blobs controlled by a single will, the instinct of each one to reach the green area where water is, as if something tells them it had just appeared by magic.

We descend by Magdal Shams along a road that at first traverses orchards, then bare rocky land, towards the demilitarised zone. At a scale of 1:100,000 the Survey of Israel maps are accurate and easy to follow, though the paper they are printed on is poor. In dictatorships such maps are never available, either to tourists or their own people, being regarded as military secrets.

South-east towards Kuneitra the landscape is featureless, except for isolated (and probably fortified) hills. We give a middle-aged soldier a lift into the Hula Valley, which is as Biblically fertile as if thirty inches of gentle rain fell over it every year. The road goes level for some miles, then descends abruptly for a few hundred feet, scene of the Israeli counterattack against the Assyrian cohorts in October 1973.

After the soldier gets out we park for an hour by the large ponds of fish farms. David goes bird spotting, and claims five new sightings. The most common tree is the fast-growing eucalyptus – tall, robust, scented and leafy. In the intense heat we drink tea out of the flask, eat biscuits, and rest.

From the high ground near Rosh Pinna, Lake Tiberias (Yam Kinneret) appears, misty and glass-like. After a day's run of 130 kilometres we reach Ginnosar and book in at the kibbutz guest house. I take off my soaking vest and shirt, and swim in the lake.

The bathing place is fenced off, and campers are already lying on opened bedrolls, glad of any spot to sleep at this time of year. The water is shallow, and a plastic bag wraps itself around my ankle as if wanting to get taken out of the water. Maybe it wasn't such a miracle that someone could walk on its surface.

213

Dinner at seven begins with soup, then a kind of warm sausage roll in gravy, followed by somewhat tasteless turkey, and ending with a cornflour mousse of indeterminate fruit flavouring. Still, we are famished, and it is pleasant enough.

At half-past eight we go upstairs to an hour's lecture illustrated by slides, on the origins and aims of the kibbutz. Ginnosar was founded in 1937, for about a hundred people, and now it has a population of six hundred. Cotton, bananas and dairy farming provide the main income, also fishing and tourism. In 1937 there wasn't a single tree, and thousands of tons of stones had to be shifted. Each kibbutz can give a similar account of its beginnings, and for four per cent of Israelis who live in them the life seems as near ideal as can be got in this world. Even so, Ginnosar, like other such settlements, loses twenty per cent of its young each year, when they leave for different places and lifestyles.

While I am studying Zev Vilnay's guidebook, an American family of parents and three children at the next table are going through a 'consciousness raising session' after having heard the lecture on kibbutz life. The father tells the children that on getting back home they ought to share the chore of washing the dishes after a meal, instead of just drifting off to 'do their own thing'. He invites the wife and children, in a sombre strident tone, to comment on his suggestion.

The children say how much better it is to do what they want to do instead of having to think about the washing-up. The father, in countering this argument, is aided by his wife, though she speaks only at intervals, when she can get a word in edgeways, and out of loyalty and a sense of duty to him in front of the children, as if she can't really believe what is taking place – or perhaps, from hard experience, she can. He goes on rebutting their tentatively put objections, hectoring in such a way that the six-year-old boy, after putting in his few feeble alternatives, mostly at the way things are going, starts to cry. He doesn't quite know what it is all about, only that his father is angry because no one had ever thought of helping mother with washing the dishes at home.

The smarter (and braver) eight-year-old girl suggests that to her knowledge the father has never done any washing-up, either. This doesn't go down well, and he harangues them more angrily, finally walking away to the bar accompanied by his overweight twelve-year-old son, who has said little because he knows he will never move a finger to wash the damned dishes anyway. Judging by the companionable manner in which he and his father walk off together, he seems to be his favourite.

Up at seven after a good night's rest, we go to Tiberias which, after the calm oasis of the kibbutz, is hot and noisy. Walking along the main street, we shop for a loaf and a water melon, then make space out of town to the hot springs by the lake side. We sit at a vacant table in the air-conditioned spa building, drink mint tea and read the *Jerusalem Post*, while large middle-aged ladies in plain frocks walk to and fro.

I change $50, then go back through town and find the road to Nazareth, turning right on a track towards Zefat. Pick up an Arab man and a boy from the roadside. The boy gets off at Eilabun, and the man intends to catch a bus that had just stopped there. We see the bus drive off without him, and he is so angry he throws a stone. He misses. The driver didn't see him, so it's nobody's fault. I pick the man up again and chase the bus along a winding and unfamiliar road, unable to go very fast, whereas the bus driver has obviously done the route every day for years and can belt along. But I overtake at the crossroads just as it's about to turn – and transfer our passenger safely onto it.

We are rewarded by a view of Maghan, flat-roofed houses spreading over the hillside and blending perfectly with it. At the main Acre-Safed road we give a lift to an old Druze gent; so frail is he that I nip out to open the door. He shows much gratitude, and walks off towards the houses.

Safed is hot and crowded, but we find an ice-cream place that a friend in Yamit told us was the best in town. David thinks it rather indifferent, but I can't say because I never eat the stuff. Make our way down steps to the artists' quarter, in parts somewhat ruinous, and visit three of the famous synagogues, each with their own simple and reverent atmosphere, thinking there seems every point in preserving them. A tourist group in one is lectured in fair English by the beadle, who in his cap and shirt looks like a Soviet engine driver. The guide with the group tells his flock the kind of joke that doesn't go down well in such a place.

We leave town, and map-read our way a few miles north to a picnic spot among the trees at Fort Biriyya. Pine cones cracking in the heat sound as if invisible fire is spreading. A man sleeps beside the open door of his car with the radio on, and I think I would only want to be a dictator in order to declare war on unnecessary noise.

The place is bad for flies, and pine trees always house many insects. On finishing our flask of tea filled at the kibbutz, I play the swaddie and get the stove going to make more, then sit on the car step to write in my diary. David wanders the woods looking for butterflies, and Ruth reads *The Odessa File*, our only novel at the moment, which David has just finished. He comes back, unable to hunt in such heat, and we talk about the book, filling in the background on Nazism and anti-Semitism, though as he says, he knows most of it already.

Leaving the grove at half-past four, we go back to the Safed crossroads and give two riflemen a lift to Rosh Pinna, through burning heat on the descent. I haven't felt the heat so much before, not even in Sinai. Dramatic views of the window-glass sea, and the crestlines of hills beyond hills in a southerly direction.

We give two Swiss girls a ride to the synagogue at Capernaum, but we are twenty minutes late, and the place is closed already, so we get into the car and go back to Tabigha, hoping to see the peacock mosaics on the church floor. The Swiss girls are afraid to go in because a notice says you must not do so wearing shorts. I tell them to have a look, anyway, which they do. David, also wearing shorts, doesn't let the notice influence him.

We leave the girls at the main road because they are going north to Rosh Pinna. About five we are back in our air-conditioned oasis. Candles are lit on the table for supper, plus half a bottle of red wine between us. We wonder if it's a festival, but are told it is not. The buffet is an opulent array of delicious food, and I eat too much. David has an upset stomach, due either to last night's meal, or the heat of the day, which at three o'clock was 107 degrees. Ruth takes him to hear the lecture about the kibbutz, while I sit in the lobby looking at maps and road routes. We did 105 kilometres today. We go to bed at eleven, to find David already asleep.

Next morning, a pressure of heat against the face, and I want to get back above sea level. We give a lift to two women and three children as far as Tiberias. They pack the car, but couldn't be left by the roadside. We only hope we're not ruining the national bus trade. We go to the south shore of Yam Kinneret, through camping sites and banana plantations of Deganya Aleph, a kibbutz that has a natural history museum, and a library of 45,000 volumes. The entomological specimens interest David, but he isn't feeling well, so does not get the best out of them, though the curator is kind and helpful. The museum was formed in 1941 from the nucleus of Beth Gordon's collection of animals, plants and mineralogical exhibits. The museum is unique, and there is also a meteorological station in the village.

In the 1948 War of Independence the kibbutz was almost destroyed in a Syrian tank attack aimed at the Jezreel Valley. One of the Renault tanks that penetrated the perimeter defences is now a monument, on the spot where it was knocked out by a Molotov cocktail.

We drive up the hills, away from Lake Tiberias and stop at Afula to buy cold drinks, and some tobacco. Turn south towards Jenin. Beyond Jezreel a tall but thinning column of blackish smoke hovers over a field. It is obviously a bomb explosion and we wonder if some kind of fighting hasn't broken out. Still driving along the straight road I hear the roar of a fighter plane, see it come down to about fifty feet and cross in front of us. Over the field a black object falls from its fuselage. The plane sheers up and out of sight. The object hits the ground, and a mass of flame spreads outwards, black smoke at the edges, seeming like fire or napalm two hundred yards away.

I slow the car almost to a halt so as to see more of what's going on. Wooden observation 'hides' along the road face the area of the explosion, which leads me to assume we are passing – if not actually going through – a bombing range. Another fighter comes in on its training run, this time directly over the car, so that the sky seems to rip open with noise. David wants to know what sort of a plane it is, and I say I think it's a Kfir. Neither this one nor the next drops bombs. Perhaps they have seen our car, and don't want to take the risk of hitting us. Or maybe they prefer a second run for greater accuracy. Ruth is a bit startled so I trundle reluctantly on. David regrets this, but is glad we are passing at such a time. I feel almost as if we are the object of an attack, though if so they can hardly fail to get us. Another bomb falls in the middle of the wisp of smoke that lingers from the one before. I can read Hebrew signposts, but must have missed that which warned of bombing practice up ahead – if there was one.

We go through Jenin and into Samaria, a closely cultivated area of fruit and olive trees. Boys stand by the roadside selling baskets of figs, but I have always disliked fresh figs, so don't want to buy any. One kid is so disappointed or angry that he steps into the road, shouts 'Jew!' and throws a stone, which misses. If he hadn't meant it as an insult, I would have taken it as a compliment.

Shekhem, or Nablus, home of the Samaritans, is a beautiful city seen from afar, its many parts seeming to hang on various hillsides. Beyond, the scenery opens out even more attractively, mostly vast plantations of olive groves, and forests rising smokily over mountain slopes. After Ramallah we are on the motorway to Jerusalem, and get there by half-past two, having driven 165 kilometres. At the sight of David's Tower, we know we are home again.

Her Victory: *A Novel Born or Made?*

People now and again ask how the plot of a novel comes to mind. Before it does, I say, there is a ream of paper or a large notebook of unlined pages before me and, between fingers and thumb of my left hand, the smallest word processor in the world: a fountain pen. I hold it high in order to amuse.

Having written 22 novels I see no reason to change, either to make the work easier or increase the rate of production. Time and motion study is not for me. Some years ago I bought an Amstrad machine so as to answer yes when asked by another writer at a party if I used a word processor. The words grated, because the only word processor I know is the brain, but £500 seemed a small price to pay for not putting up with half an hour's proselytising on how much work they saved.

I don't dislike the benefits of technology, but an electric typewriter with an erasure mechanism is as far as I care to go in lightening the labour. Otherwise a state-of-the-art short-wave communications radio on my desk acts as a sort of therapy when I tune in and read Morse code, a source of information and occasional enlightenment from stations as far apart as Cape Town and Nakhodka. My fascination with machines dates from factory days, and I drive a car with pleasure, so technology is good only when its accomplishments demand some skill of my own.

The components of the word processor were scattered over the floor as if a mechanical mastodon had vomited in disgust at the defiant refilling of my pen, and the soft-footed sound of a typewriter. The gimmick was eventually gathered together, put into the car, and locked in the back room of our country house, while assuming I might tackle its mysteries when a free month came between novels.

I would then go on to explain, at a reading or talk, that to write a novel you need observation, memory and imagination. Throw in a talent for narration, if you care to. Ten or more years ago, hoping to find out where fiction came from, a university in California (I forget the name) posted a document to various novelists, its scores of questions needing the best part of a month to deal with. I thought to let humour loose by responding as if my answers came from someone called Arnold Bennett or Virginia Woolf (or both) but finally slung the sheets into a waste basket, wanting the source of fiction to remain in its remote and secret glen – or wherever it lurked. I felt unable, in any case, to comment on a process so close to my life-long obsession. Such exploration was the critic's work and not the novelist's, the two being separated by a gap of Grand Canyon dimensions.

I write stories rather than fill in forms, though a narrative could be made out of how I began a novel called *Her Victory*, an explanation that, in a back-handed way, might answer some of the queries from that place of learning in California.

My home for thirty years has been in the Notting Hill district of West London, half a mile from the Portobello Road market, with its antique stalls and lively population round about. Every Friday morning I take the car as close as it can be parked to where fruit and vegetables are sold from barrows along the kerb, and buy whatever organic provisions are needed for the week.

On a mistily cold morning of May 1976 (the month was long recalled as November, due to the inclement weather, but my diary reveals otherwise), I was in a queue to buy bananas and oranges. A woman walking along the pavement could have been missed had I been pointing out to the stallholder what was wanted, or paying, or stowing the goods into my basket, because she was only in view for a few seconds.

Other people were passing, and though her face may not have been as interesting to them, a photo flash ignited chemicals of the right compound to make a firm imprint. After unloading the baskets in the kitchen at home, I went into my room and wrote:

'She has fine features, and carried a shopping bag. Not that she was particularly startling, but I noticed that she was fine boned in the face, and pale, and her teeth were even, and a little bigger than average or what you might expect from such a face.'

She had neither laughed nor otherwise opened her mouth, so the mention of teeth could suggest that my imagination was already working.

'But it wasn't so much detail that impressed me as a certain look in her eyes. There was a feeling she had been carefully nurtured and brought up, that she was fairly well educated – may even have had a degree – but that she'd gone through a time of adjustment and stress, and was still partly in it. There had been hard times, unexpected times, perhaps months of sacrifice for some kind of ideal to do with love. Her eyes had a look of wonder that she was still surviving, a sense of pain that she was only three-quarters through and didn't yet know whether she would finally get to the other side. By no means a raw and too obvious expression, it was plain and noticeable. She did not look unhappy, nor had she been made hard-faced by whatever it was she had gone through, but her spirit had been marked and, if anything, it made her look more interesting than before it all happened.'

I left such confusing observations and went back to a novel in which she could have no place. Ten months later, much of that work being finished, and wanting a change, I turned the pages of my notebook, bemused at so many dull and useless items, till coming to that about the woman seen during a May morning as meteorologically uncertain as the month in which Izaak Walton talked so eloquently to an angler friend while sheltering from the rain.

Relishing the vacuity of idleness, I didn't want her shadow bothering me, but she wouldn't go back into the fog of the unconscious, remaining for whatever reason an impertinent solidarity, as if only a week had passed since writing 'whatever it was she had gone through'. The question as to how she had come to be going by the stall at which I did my shopping intrigued me, as did the trouble she had obviously endured.

The face worked on me, demanding more than a few notes about her. Not having an overcoat pointed to a psychological aspect, and more disturbance than at first assumed, which so increased my interest that I had no alternative but to try and explain how she had come to be walking down the Portobello Road at that particular time.

Pamela would fit as a first name, and I made her forty years old. Born and brought up in Nottingham – where else? – she had married at twenty, more because it was the thing to do than from being in love, as she was to remind herself when too late. Her husband George, a skilled and intelligent mechanic, built up a workshop and business whose machines turned out small items that larger firms wouldn't handle. He made enough money for them to buy a comfortable bungalow on the outskirts of the city.

A year after the wedding the birth of a son created a buffer between her and George that kept them together longer than it should. As individuals they were difficult, as a couple certainly unsuited, and Pam often thought of leaving him. When she was forty their son went away to technical college in Manchester, leaving them in the explosive box of their dwelling.

The novel opens when Pam comes down to make George's breakfast, over which he taunts her, unable to put up with her permanent look of unhappiness, for which he can see no reason. She has never appreciated the easy life he worked so hard to maintain, and his sneering reiteration of this leads to a more than bitter quarrel, in which she picks up a bread knife intending to maim or kill. A strong and agile man, he knocks the weapon aside and then, disturbed by her set purpose, does his best to calm her with more kindly words, before driving away to his workshop.

Alone, she thinks of spreading paraffin and sending the house up in flames, but packs two suitcases with her most-needed possessions, and telephones for a taxi. In the middle of the city

222

she draws the few hundred pounds from her personal account, and gets on a train to London.

After a few uncertain days in a bed and breakfast place near St Pancras Station she realises that her money won't last forever, that cheaper accommodation and some kind of job must be found. Following up advertisements in the *Evening Standard*, she traipses over much of London, finally deciding on a furnished room in the Notting Hill area. I see her walking down the Portobello Road on that bleak Friday morning in May, going back to the refuge of her squalid habitation after being interviewed for a job she didn't get, which accounted for the uncertainties of her expression.

This hundred-page account of Pam's early life and the rupture of her marriage took five weeks to write. 'After dinner,' said a diary of that year, 'I did another nine pages of my novel, and corrected them. I still don't know where it is going, but I don't need to as it is still so early on. It seems to be about a woman who, after a desert of a marriage, sets out on a quest to find herself spiritually, to try and discover, if she can, or if I can make her, what her relationship is to the universe, to society, and maybe to herself – perhaps, finally, to God.'

Metaphysics don't promise good storytelling, so nothing further came to take Pam into her new life. I typed what had been done, and put the sheets into an envelope.

Preoccupied with another novel, I still looked for her on weekly visits to the market, as if to glean clues regarding the life she must be leading. Perhaps she would be wearing more stylish clothes, even sporting a briefcase, or be arm in arm with a man, or talking to a woman friend. Pictures began to move and intrigue, yet I didn't see her. Maybe she stayed aloof out of reproach, scornful at my inability to continue with the book she deserved. Was it necessary to see that she was enduring the pain of a strange existence in order for me to believe? Wasn't imagination supposed to have eyes?

Eighteen months went by before reading the papers again, then the lock snapped and the door opened onto Pam's further experiences. I hand-wrote those previously typed pages into a ledger, revising as I went along, to create a tuning fork for the quality of the rest, and at the end of that task, in a haze almost of unknowing, but with infinite clarity as the pen moved, it was at last clear how the story must go on.

It is easier to start a novel than to end one, as it is in life to begin something than get out of what trouble was half-knowingly gone into, and this applied to Pam on leaving her husband, and to me after taking up her story. To set the process going, one person has to meet another and, when Pam did, a relationship began, out of which came conflict, and therefore a story. People are pulled in as a magnet attracts iron filings, and something happens.

Put into contact with strangers, facing despair and peril, Pamela became different to the person she had been when first taken up. No novel succeeds if the people in it have not to a large extent changed by the end, otherwise there would be little purpose in giving them so much thought and labour. Though my heroine, as she now was, might not fundamentally alter, those attitudes and responses that she had been unaware of, reluctant as they had been to show, now began to influence the course of her life. A pitiable refugee from an impossible marriage, who had abandoned family and home ground forever, she was to meet more cosmopolitan people than those of her previous existence.

By the end she had given birth to a daughter, though without remarrying, and was to know more about herself than ever before. The novel was different to any other of mine in that all the movements of the plot were initiated by women.

'A novel is like travelling,' George Sand wrote to Flaubert, 'but it's what happens next that's important.' So Pamela met people I hardly expect to see myself, demanding a part in her story. It often happens that people do – the psyche being densely inhabited – as when on the eightieth page of *The Death of William Posters* my hero, Frank Dawley, saunters into a village pub and gets into casual talk with someone at the bar. The stranger not only influenced all further chapters of the novel but, with the members of his family, populated two more volumes that turned it into a trilogy.

A beginning is made with one person, though it is no guarantee that the novel will go on. People can turn into ghosts impossible to hold, refuse to cooperate and set the narrative going, leaving you with nothing more than a short story, if you are lucky – or dextrous. I once began what seemed to be a story, and stopped when five hundred pages had turned it into a picaresque novel. Uncertainty creates a field of energy that decides what shape and length the work will be, leaving the writer with little to say.

The writing goes on for month after month, with many stops and starts, and times when weariness or lack of invention (or both) seems to freeze the ink, and you think that much of what's been done should be slung into the fire. 'I'm writing this novel, or whatever it is,' said my diary, 'in an uncompromising way, just going on and on, without thought of form or presentation, though this may take place when the first draft is finished. I've yet to know what the hell I'm doing.'

Pessimism can bring on hypochondria that influences the inexorable work of guiding the narrative and tending the style. I cough and half choke over the multiplicity of uncertain directions, wondering whether I'm getting asthma, or if my lungs are rotting, or my kidneys packing in, or how I will go on writing if struck blind. A painful stomach ache may signify ulcers, or something more sinister that has to be ignored for seven years so as to tell me whether or not the affliction is fatal.

A beneficial walk in the middle of London brings me back to lunch, and an hour's sleep. Three small glasses of ice-cold vodka at supper turns everything rosy again, and sets me writing till midnight. Mistaking euphoria for inspiration, I might do ten pages, though such an influence rarely results in good work.

Writing novels may be a way of searching for a character recognisable as myself. If ever encountered, he might chase away the demons that won't let me rest, release me from seeing *myself* walking along the Portobello Road, back from talking to Pam and learning more about her life, going home to fill another page of my notebook, before realising with chagrin that it is myself I see, and that I shall never write again. Such an egomaniacal

225

encounter makes it difficult to believe that the self I inhabit is the real me, as I scratch away with a pen to create people who take me over so decisively.

The rabbi of medieval Prague made a *golem* from dust and water to do those chores on the Sabbath forbidden to a pious Jew, and when the *golem* went out of control and began to endanger people, the wise rabbi turned the creature back into harmless mud. A writer can't do that. His *golem* is recalcitrant, has a mind, and may never go away. Nor does the writer have a Sabbath, yet hopes that God will forgive him for taking over the souls of whoever wanders into the difficult symphony of his novel.

Such puppeteering enables you to know your people, male or female, to become them while working the strings. They dance in the country of your imagination, driven before the winds of fate like dandelion fluff, at times held still long enough for you to fall in love and turn them into words. However awkward, disputatious or villainous, you become as familiar with them as they are with themselves.

Reaching the last chapters of a book, I am reluctant to finish, want the people to stay and not leave me alone, in spite of the work demanded. But the novel must come to an end, and I hope my well-used characters will feel satisfied with conclusions so carefully arranged. In the future one of them might so vividly come to mind that I wonder whether I actually met him or her in real life, then feel relieved that whoever it was had merely insinuated a way into my novel at a time convenient for us both, and that they had no one to blame but themselves for the fate handed out. Symbiosis as a state of mind, or several minds, can go no further.

The completed ramshackle manuscript is like an air liner that has travelled by various zig-zags from A towards Z, now about to join the circuit of the arrival airport. My air-traffic control experience comes into play: as captain of their fate (but not my own), I put the flaps down and lock the undercarriage into position at the sight of the runway, reducing speed so as not to alarm the passengers, and make such a smooth landing that they hardly know they are back on earth, and can go their different ways.

I hope they are settled comfortably forever, but on a pitch dark night before the most sombre of dawns one might return from where he was packed off to be buried, and climb through the window wielding a glinting razor-sharp butcher's knife, to demand with bloodshot eyes and a trembling lower lip (with a scab on it) how I could ever have done such a thing: 'You put me through situations neither deserved nor expected, and I gave you good service in your novel, without any thanks, and you left me in that parlous situation. I've been in torment ever since. Why did you do it?'

Sweating as after a nightmare, I feel no guilt about his (or her) fate. Immortality exists for pope, king or pop star only insofar as they are remembered, and invented people in novels live for as long as readers are interested in their stories, so they have no more to complain about than flesh-and-blood people on whom their actions might be based.

The 472 pages of the first draft were finished in five months, and for some reason I put the time of the day after the last sentence: 10.40 in the evening. For a few weeks the closely written sheets came up clean and neat from the typewriter. Reading the book one night over a few drinks – a time of light-headed deception, when anything written seems more than satisfactory – I thought little else needed to be done, but on looking again under a cold sky after breakfast the pen began amending and cutting here and there, till it was obvious that every line needed revision, the process like that of a sculptor who must carve a group of figures from a block of stone: he hammers and chips for weeks until, little by little, they are recognisable enough to be further worked on and refined.

Most of what had been optimistically scrawled turned out to be uneven and often lifeless, some parts better than others, but each sentence had to be brought up to the standard of those which were lucid. Pages blackened with multitudes of corrections were almost impossible to read, and a third draft, of 728 pages, was finished on 1 January 1981.

I was then convinced that it was perfect. Please give me a pat on the back. I've done it, I can relax, a feeling of relief and accomplishment, nothing but to make a parcel and send it in. Another reading, however, showed almost the same situation as before, in that scores of adjustments thought unnecessary on the previous scanning had to be made. The aim was a flawless narrative that would let any reader assume that the novel had been done straight off, no trouble at all, in those hours when the writer was not carousing in the nearest pub or café.

Such work takes far more time than the first penned draft, an unremitting application making me say I will never write another novel, to swear as the months go by that the process is destroying my sanity, while secretly admitting (though not altogether convinced) that it's easier than working in a factory or labouring to build a motorway. A novel must be ground into submission, no matter what the effort. Writers are divided between those who choose words with the greatest care, and those who let the words choose them.

I begrudged all social life, and fought off every interruption, though a reading tour of Switzerland, arranged long before, allowed a couple of days contemplating the world from the peace of an alpine meadow.

The final draft of *Her Victory*, of 781 pages, dated 16 July 1981, was lightly corrected and sent to a typist because I couldn't face it any more. Further alterations would only make it worse and, after a last check of every jot and tittle, I put the clean typescript into a plastic bag and took it to my agent's office, feeling like Jean-Jacques Rousseau laying a foundling babe on the orphanage steps, screaming its guts out for tender loving care. To use another metaphor, I cast my bread upon the waters in the hope that it would come back spread with jam of a high fruit content.

My agent read the book, with little enthusiasm, but sent it to Jonathan Cape Limited, who had published a previous collection of my stories. In the meantime I went on a 140-mile ten-day trek around the Kent coast, to write about a footpath called The Saxon Shore Way, hoping to do justice to the photographs of Fay Godwin. Walking day after day in rain or sun was soothing. My small rucksack of seven or eight kilos contained maps, binoculars, compass, a spare shirt and underwear, a miniature tape recorder in which to speak notes, and a pocket edition of *Great Expectations* to escape to in strange rooms at night.

A message on my return said would I please go to the offices at Jonathan Cape and talk about the novel, the implication being that some changes needed to be made. They wanted me to sit at a table with an editor and, in a friendly manner – maybe the firm would provide a bottle or two of wine to ease our work – decide what to cut out, what to switch here and there, how to soften the emphasis of certain events, perhaps even to add incidents not previously imagined. We would rewrite the book between us, mixing our styles to make it acceptable not only to the publisher's policy but to those who might eventually buy a copy.

Being a more experienced novelist than any editor, I asked for the book to be sent back, which it duly was, with no acerbic feelings on either side. Some writers are not unhappy at having their books tinkered into a final version (which should have more than one name on the title page) though there's no way of telling whether such a process sells more copies than if the work had been left alone. While one editor will say one thing, another will suggest the opposite, and in the end only the writer's decision matters. My first novel, *Saturday Night and Sunday Morning*, went to several publishers, and different alterations were suggested by each, but when the book came out as written it sold well enough and is still in print.

Just as I had been tempted to respond to the questionnaire from California as if I were someone else (such mischief a diversion from the serious work of writing) one might wonder whether I did not make up seeing the woman on the Portobello Road. Well, she was real enough, but the rest of what happened was invented, came to mind, you could say, out of nowhere, much like the character Albert Handley in *The Death of William Posters*. Nothing succeeds until it has been refashioned into the truth, and Pam was merely a device to jump-start me into making a believable story. A writer is nothing if not an ant-hill of ambiguities.

In novels and stories I avoid politics and pointing out social injustice, preferring to define character and let the conditions in which he or she lives explain whatever plight they feel burdened by. It would be futile and dishonest to encourage the victims of misery to throw off their limitations by wishing to destabilise the high standards of bourgeois culture, which is the only one open to their aspirations, if they are given any, and certainly the only one wherein a writer can feel comfortable. A so-called message is more powerful by being concealed as if not to be there.

To give the impression by the end of a story of such irredeemable human behaviour to the reader that there seems nothing else to do except commit suicide out of despair is not my purpose either. I stay within the tradition of the English novel, where whatever is new in form or content or language is close to what has gone before – evolution rather than revolution.

The most effective and humane propaganda is art, and if no man is born an artist, as Izaak Walton avers (I have just re-read his book, so refer to him again) then my persistence in becoming one was helped when the woman on the Portobello Road was lifted from the grey drizzle of a May morning and made the heroine of my novel.

Her Victory was published as written by HarperCollins in 1982, and by Franklin Watts in the United States, and produced by Books on Tape in 1985; so many in hardback and paperback years after writing the first details of that unknown woman in my notebook. A German translation under the title of *Die Frau auf der Brücke* came out in 1989, from Gustav Lubbe Verlag.

I still occasionally think of that mysterious woman on Friday mornings while standing by a market stall, hoping to see her and find out whether the life she went on to live conformed to what I had written. Nearly 25 years have gone by, so she would be unrecognisable anyway, and who she really was, I'll never know.